LONGMAN LITERATURE

Pygmalion

be returned on or before

Bernard Shaw

Editor: Jacqueline Fisher

LONGMAN

Contents

☐ The writer on writing

Shaw on drama

In 1898 the forty-two-year-old George Bernard Shaw published his first volume of plays, containing *Widowers' Houses*, *The Philanderer* and *Mrs Warren's Profession*. These plays tend to attack a lot of what Shaw felt were the bad elements in his society and so from the start of his playwriting career Shaw built up a reputation for making his audiences feel uncomfortable watching his plays. Above all he wanted to make people *think* at the theatre rather than just sit watching something quite forgettable.

To make sure actors represented his views correctly and so that anyone reading his plays understood exactly what he meant, Shaw preceded every play by a Preface which gave his views on the play's themes and his aims in writing the play in the first place. These Prefaces were sometimes as long (or even longer in the case of *Androcles and the Lion*) as the plays themselves, although most of the plays were written long before the Prefaces. Shaw intended each Preface and each play to be a complete work in itself.

This is how Shaw started his Preface to that first 1898 volume:

> There is an old saying that if a man has not fallen in love before forty, he had better not fall in love after. I long ago perceived that this rule applied to many other matters as well: for example, to the writing of plays; and I made a rough memorandum for my own guidance that unless I could produce at least half a dozen plays before I was forty I had better let playwriting alone. It was not so easy to comply with this provision as might be supposed. Not that I lacked the dramatist's gift…[but] I had no taste for what is called popular art, no respect for popular morality, no belief in popular religion, no admiration for popular heroics.

> As a humane person I detested violence and slaughter, whether in war, sport, or the butcher's yard. I was a Socialist, detesting our scramble for money, and believing in equality as the only possible permanent basis of social organisation, discipline, good manners, and selection of fit persons for high functions.

Apart from continuing with an account of his history as a writer, Shaw also explained why he called this first volume *Plays Unpleasant* (at the same time he published a companion volume as *Plays Pleasant*):

> *The reason is pretty obvious: their dramatic power is used to force the spectator to face unpleasant facts. No doubt all plays which deal sincerely with humanity must wound the monstrous conceit [imagination] which it is the business of romance to flatter. But here we are confronted...with those social horrors which arise from the fact that the average homebred Englishman, however honorable and goodnatured he may be in his private capacity, is a citizen, a wretched creature who...will shut his eyes to the most villainous abuses if the remedy threatens to add another penny to the rates and taxes which he has to be half cheated, half coerced into paying.*

It is hardly surprising, therefore, that Shaw was labelled a dramatist of *ideas*. He insisted that plays *had* to be about ideas – *the drama can never be anything more* – and he thought nothing of writing pages in trying to find remedies for any problems which came to mind.

In the Preface of 1903 to one of his longest plays, *Man and Superman*, Shaw addressed his words to Arthur Bingham Walkley, a respected theatre critic, and again described the kind of plays he was trying to write:

> *It is your favourite jibe at me that what I call drama is nothing but explanation. But you must not expect me to adopt your ways: you must take me as I am, a reasonable, patient, consistent, apologetic, laborious person....I have a conscience; and conscience is always explanatory....My conscience is the genuine pulpit article: it annoys me to see people comfortable when they ought to be uncomfortable; and I insist on making them think....If you don't like my preaching you must lump it. I really cannot help it.*

It is quite clear that Shaw was prepared to go against public opinion and even offend people as long as he could write what he believed to be the right thing. Shaw could write masses on anything – from how a government should run a country to the shape of a character's moustache in one of his plays!

Born in Ireland in 1856, and leaving school at the age of fifteen to work as an office boy in a Land Agent's firm, Shaw wrote four novels (which he had difficulty publishing), over fifty plays of varying lengths, hundreds of political, literary and economic pamphlets, critical essays which became books in their own right, and what must have amounted to thousands of letters. He also spoke to every organisation and society possible as he claimed to have an opinion on everything – on being a vegetarian or a teetotaler, on animal rights or human rights, on the language both spoken and written, on politics or domestic matters, on the theatre or personal hobbies.

At his death at the age of ninety-four in 1950 many theatres observed a two-minute silence and the lights of New York's Broadway were switched off as a mark of respect for a man who had become a British institution, recognised just by those famous initials GBS.

His career as a playwright started well after his move to London in 1876 to join his mother, who had left Shaw's father and followed her singing teacher to London. Following a time of unemployment, unsuccessful novel writing and almost non-stop reading of all kinds of literary and political works (including Karl Marx's *Das Kapital*), he started reviewing art, music and drama in famous journals of the time – *The Pall Mall Gazette*, *The World*, *The Star* and *The Saturday Review*. Only in 1884 did he begin to write plays.

It became clear that he wanted to write a different kind of play from the Victorian plays which he saw in London and which he considered to be trivial and without meaning:

> The playgoer...wants to drink, to smoke, to change the spectacle, to get rid of the middle-aged actor and actress who are boring him, and to see shapely young dancing girls and acrobats doing more amusing things.... In short he wants the music hall.... And so we must conclude that the theatre is a place which people can endure only when they forget themselves.... Imagine, then, the result of conducting theatres on the principle of appealing exclusively to the instinct of self-gratification in people without brains or heart. That is how they were conducted whilst I was writing about them; and that is how they nearly killed me.
>
> Preface to Three Plays for Puritans

Shaw felt Theatre should be *much* more important:

> The theatre is growing in importance as a social organ. Bad theatres are as mischievous as bad schools or bad churches...The truth is that dramatic invention is the first effort of man to become intellectually conscious...the national

importance of the theatre will be as unquestioned as that of the Army..., the Church, the law and the schools.

Preface to Plays Pleasant

Clearly, Shaw had ideas for the theatre and he held up as an example the great nineteenth-century Norwegian dramatist Henrik Ibsen whose plays such as *Hedda Gabler* and *Ghosts* began to be performed towards the end of that century, causing a sensation among audiences. In Shaw's book *The Quintessence of Ibsenism* he tried to show the public that drama *must* be concerned with conflict and ideas – nothing less would do. Shaw felt that Ibsen's influence was beginning to seep into the English playwright's mind:

Playwrights who formerly only compounded plays according to the received prescriptions for producing tears or laughter are already taking their profession seriously to the full extent of their capacity, and venturing more and more to substitute the incidents and catastrophes of spiritual history for [that is, instead of] the swoons, surprises, discoveries, murders, duels, assassinations, and intrigues which are the commonplaces of the theatre at present. What is wanted is the entire abolition of the censorship and the establishment of Free Art .

Shaw was a man with strong convictions about the theatre and a hatred for what he felt was unimportant Drama: he wanted to be considered as a realist in his writing. Replying to the famous writer and critic William Archer, in 1895 Shaw wrote in *Our Theatres in the Nineties* (1895):

For him [William Archer] there is illusion in the theatre: for me there is none...for me the play is not the thing, but its thought, its purpose, its feeling and its execution.... To him acting, like scene-painting, is merely a means to an end, that end being to enable him to make believe. To me the play is only the means, the end being the expression of feeling by the arts of the actor, the poet, the musician. Anything that makes this expression more vivid is so much to the good for me.

Shaw on language

Throughout his life Shaw fought long and difficult battles to change the spelling system of the English language. He thought that most English spelling was ridiculous because it had nothing to do with the way words were pronounced.

Shaw wrote more on practical grounds rather than with regard for the historical development of the language. To make his point he gave a famous and clever illustration: he took the word FISH and claimed that it could easily be spelt as GHOTI. This was his explanation: GH together could be pronounced as the last two letters in the word lau<u>gh</u>; O would have the sound of the first vowel in the word w<u>o</u>men; TI would be pronounced as the t in the word na<u>t</u>ion. So when the letters were all put together they would spell:

GH the F sound in lau<u>gh</u>
O the I sound in w<u>o</u>men
TI the SH sound in na<u>t</u>ion

Using this example Shaw wanted to show that the English language was in need of great reform and the only way to succeed, he thought, would be to have a new phonetic alphabet.

In *Pygmalion* Shaw makes his main male character a professor of phonetics. Phonetics is the study of the sound of language and the science of putting down all the different sounds into a system of written signs. The International Phonetic Association has devised a phonetic alphabet although some of the signs do not look at all like letters from the English language. Look at these lines written in the Universal Phonetic Alphabet where each phonetic letter represents a sound. This is followed by the same lines in ordinary spelling:

ənd ðɛn maɪ hɑːt wɪð plɛʒə fɪlz
ənd dɑːnsɪz wɪð ðə dafədɪlz.

And then my heart with pleasure fills
And dances with the daffodils.

Wordsworth

With a completely new phonetic alphabet Shaw felt problems could be solved such as those created by the existence of words that contained the same combination of letters but were pronounced differently, for example: *ought, though, thorough, trough, Slough*. It was silly, Shaw thought, to have the same letters all pronounced in different ways. There was a similar problem with letters such as PH and F, C and K, SH and T. There was in existence a Simplified Spelling Society (run by Daniel Jones and Sir Isaac Pitman) which wanted to perfect an alternative alphabetic system but Shaw wanted to go one stage further and base an alphabet on many more letters than we use now:

> We cannot get away from phonetic spelling, because spelling is as necessarily and inevitably phonetic as moisture is damp....Unless we adopt a system of Chinese ideographs, and learn by heart a separate arbitrary symbol of every word in the dictionary we must spell phonetically.

Shaw thought that spelling and pronounciation would suffer:

> If we will not spell as we pronounce, the world will end by pronouncing as we spell.

In his will, Shaw left a large amount of money for the introduction of a new alphabet so that all the masterpieces of the English language could be transliterated (rewritten in letters of a new alphabet) and people would be able to start reading phonetically. Any new alphabet would need at least forty letters, he thought, rather than our twenty-six; in fact he worked out a system using forty-two letters.

At the beginning of *Pygmalion* Shaw tries to write the words of Eliza Doolittle phonetically and uses a symbol looking like a back to front 'e' to help him: ə. This symbol is called a SCHWA and represents a very neutral sound; about the nearest sound to it is the u in absurd, or the i in bird. Also in the play he avoids many apostrophes claiming most of them *arent* necessary; and he uses American-style spellings for some words, for example, color instead of colour.

Although Shaw's wishes were not able to be carried out, his will was important and in 1962 his play *Androcles and the Lion* was published with the Shaw Alternative Alphabet version alongside. This version does not just look like a different alphabet, it appears to be a new language.

Shaw on politics

Much of *Pygmalion* revolves around a very divided class system. One of the play's themes is close to Shaw's beliefs – that people should not be limited by their birth or environment or even their speech. It was fitting, therefore, that Shaw became one of the first members of The Fabian Society founded in 1884. This is a socialist society committed to social justice, equality, and the need for the individual to strive for some kind of perfection. Hard work, speeches and pamphlets were the order of the day to try and change the system – rather than revolution. This is how Shaw described the Society:

> The Fabian Society seeks to establish equality as the universal relation between citizens without distinction of sex, colour, occupation, age, talent, character, heredity or what not....The Fabian Society not only aims at complete political equality as between the sexes, but their economic independence. It advocates the explicit recognition by legally secured rights or payments of the value of the domestic work of women to their immediate domestic partners and to the State as housekeepers, child bearers, nurses and matrons.

It is quite apt, then, that Shaw should have as the central plot of one of his plays a bet as to whether a teacher of phonetics can teach a flower girl to pass for a duchess in six months.

Introduction

The play

Saturday, 11 April 1914, the first performance in England of *Pygmalion*, was one of the most memorable nights on the London stage. Until then Shaw had written over two dozen plays; many were praised by critics but failed to attract good audiences and so ran for limited performances. Two plays (*Press Cuttings* and *Mrs Warren's Profession*) were even banned by the Lord Chamberlain who had the power to censor or ban plays for various reasons – in Shaw's case for what was considered to be immoral content.

Pygmalion, however, became something of an overnight success and remains the outstanding example of a Shaw play to have been made into both a film (for which Shaw wrote the screenplay) and a stage musical in 1956 as the re-named *My Fair Lady,* written by Alan Jay Lerner and Frederick Loewe. This musical ran for over six and a half years in America and was in turn produced as a film starring Rex Harrison and Audrey Hepburn. How the play ever reached an audience in the first place is almost a fairy-tale in itself and needs retelling.

In one of his countless letters to the actress Ellen Terry, Shaw wrote as early as 8 September 1897 that he wanted to write a play for the famous actress Mrs Patrick Campbell to whom he referred in the letter as *that rapscallionly flower girl* and added *Caesar and Cleopatra* [another play by Shaw] *has been driven clean out of my head by a play I want to write for them* [the actor Forbes Robertson and Mrs Patrick Campbell] *in which he shall be a west end gentleman and she an east end donna in an apron and red ostrich feathers.*

Nothing happened for fifteen years but one evening while Shaw was at the St James's Theatre the actor-manager there, George Alexander, asked him to write a play for his theatre. When Shaw eventually wrote *Pygmalion*, Alexander thought it would be a great theatrical hit and went so far as to tell Shaw he would offer the actress of Shaw's choice any salary. The only problem was that Alexander refused to engage Mrs Patrick Campbell whose reputation as a temperamental and fiery actress put him off staging the play.

The correspondence between Shaw and Mrs Patrick Campbell shows that, although he wanted her for the part he wondered whether she would ever play Eliza as he wished. She too worried about how to approach the role and just hoped she would be able to please Shaw and play his *pretty slut*. It was difficult to imagine who might play Higgins – *I must have a heroic Higgins... name your man*, Shaw wrote to her in July 1912. Finally Sir Herbert Beerbohm Tree who ran His Majesty's Theatre was chosen, although while all these negotiations were taking place *Pygmalion* had been translated into German and was performed successfully in Vienna in 1913.

The London rehearsals were far from smooth and on some days they became almost violent. Tree and Shaw often disagreed about how the play should be performed. Tree wanted spectacular scenes for his audiences and was deter- mined to act with far more gestures, movements and facial expressions than Shaw wanted. Shaw and Mrs Patrick Campbell argued as well, Tree com- plaining that Mrs Patrick Campbell often became carried away with her role. Shaw once wrote of an extreme example of the problem:

> When we rehearsed this [the moment Eliza throws a pair of slippers at Higgins] I had taken care to have a very soft pair of velvet slippers provided; for I knew that Mrs P C was very dextrous, very strong and a dead shot. And, sure enough, when we reached this passage, Tree got the slippers well and truly delivered with unerring aim bang in his face. The effect was appalling. He had totally forgotten that there was any such incident in the play; and it seemed to him that Mrs P C, suddenly giving way to an impulse of diabolical wrath and hatred, had committed an unprovoked and brutal assault on him....He collapsed in tears on the nearest chair, and left me standing in amazement, whilst the entire personnel of the theatre crowded round him, explaining that the incident was part of the play.

As if that were not enough, in the middle of the final rehearsals Mrs Patrick Campbell disappeared to get married again on 6 April and did not reappear until the dress rehearsal which lasted from 10.30pm to 3am!

Letters between Shaw and Mrs PC became frantic, Shaw writing *Final Orders* just before the performance, explaining that *a good deal will depend on whether you are inspired at the last moment,* and feeling that the whole play could collapse after the third act. This letter must have concerned Mrs P C as in 1938 she recalled it with pain:

I was 25 years too old for the part... something about my figure, my movements, my voice, my natural grace annoyed you, you wanted to break it up – the girl wasn't common enough to amuse you – or it may be you wanted to take me up in your arms and kiss me, and as you couldn't you bullied me unmercifully. I was having infinite trouble with the accent,.... I have one letter of yours, written just before the first night, that would have made a weaker woman commit suicide.

Still, the play *did* reach the stage and the first night audience went mad with delight, giving Mrs Patrick Campbell one of her greatest successes. Shaw, however, left the theatre early as he could not bear the way Tree was acting (Tree had tried to suggest a romantic ending between Eliza and Higgins), and also because he felt there was too much audience laughter at the wrong place.

Shaw suddenly became financially secure with queues forming round the theatre all day to see the play; only the outbreak of the First World War prevented a long tour of the play. Although Shaw was pleased that it became successful he felt compelled to write an epilogue in case anyone should get the wrong idea about his intended ending. Perhaps the sharp interchange between Shaw and Tree sums up the different attitude towards the play from both men: when Tree rebuked Shaw for all the criticisms by telling him, *My ending makes money; you ought to be grateful*, Shaw simply replied, *Your ending is damnable; you ought to be shot*.

Critical reaction

The reviews following *Pygmalion*'s first performance in 1914 reveal the impact made by the play. Apart from writing about the production itself, newspapers concentrated on the then infamous three words with which Eliza shocks the other characters in Act 3 – *Not bloody likely* – some papers dedicating front pages or long articles to a discussion of Shaw's language. Of the play as a whole the journalists wrote:

It is just a caprice, and one of the airiest, wittiest and most impudent Mr Shaw has ever composed...the whole thing is just a burst of high spirits from an intellectual man who knows a good deal about life; and those who can thus accept it will find it a rare entertainment.

Pall Mall Gazette

A comedy of modern manners, tinged with social satire, but free from any easily recognisable didactic purpose, there runs a vein of exaggerations bordering on caricature.... Laughter reigns supreme.

Daily Mail

In a house so full of well known people that it looked as if everybody who is anybody had stayed in London over Easter on purpose to see this play, its reception was one that promised well for the new alliance between Mr Shaw and Sir Herbert Tree. The play is called a romance but those who expect passion or wedding bells will be disappointed.

Observer

A distinctly amusing first act, brisk, new, and with all its exaggeration, saved by a grain of truth. The rain is especially well done.... As for the play, it is certainly to be seen; but it will live (if it lives) for its parts rather than its whole.

The Times

The play as a whole is a joyful piece of work. There is an abundant vigour in it, and the best things come with such force, and the worst have so much spirit, and the thing marches on with such gaiety that you cannot resist it, nor do you want to. It is a great joke.... It debates and dallies with all sorts of solemn subjects in the midst of its fun. It suggests all sorts of problems, problems of our social state, of ethics, of human nature, even of scholarship, and having suggested them, drops them and goes gaily on.

Daily Telegraph

Such was the impact of the first *bloody* to be uttered on the stage that some papers had front line headlines declaring what had happened at His Majesty's Theatre – *The Pygmalion Sensation! Mrs Patrick Campbell swears on stage and cultured London roars with laughter*, headlined the *Daily Sketch* and proceeded to cover its page with pictures, comments and information about a debate between various vicars as to whether the word should have been used at all. The *Sketch* continued: *Mrs P C uttered the Unprintable Swearword at His Majesty's Theatre on Saturday night and the play stopped for a full minute till the audience had done laughing.* Some newspapers were more cynical and felt that the play became successful only because of the swear word:

O greatly daring Mr Shaw! You will be able to boast that you are the first modern dramatist to use the word on stage. But really was it worthwhile?

The Times

If you omit the swearing and the Dustman's audacious philosophy there is not much left. **Pygmalion** *will probably be a success if only for its audacity in the use of naughty swear words.*

Daily News and Leader

The critics universally praised Mrs Patrick Campbell as the *triumph* of the play and a *magnificent piece of comedy*, but Tree did not fare so well, most journalists choosing to commend Edmund Gurney who played Doolittle instead.

The *Daily Express* went one stage further than the other papers by claiming to have treated a Charing Cross flower girl called Eliza Keefe to a seat at the theatre and then printing her reaction to the play trying to capture her accent!:

Well, I've never 'ad such a night in all me natural.... Yer see, I never thought I should be so conspic – conspic – well yer knows what I mean.... I really enjoyed meself and wen I 'eard the langwidge it was quite like 'ome. I never thought as 'ow they allowed sich langwidge on the stage.... I thought Mrs P C was jist luvly, but she was not altogether wot you would call troo to life. As fer this Mr Bernard Shaw – well he finks a bloomin' sight too much ov 'imself, 'e does. There were lots of things wot reglar put me back up. Does this 'ere Mr Shaw fink flower girls are dirt?...No self-respecting flower girl would say such a word wen she was on 'er best behaviour, 'spesully if she was supposed ter be eddicated and speakin' in a drorin' room. Still, on the 'ole, I liked the play. It wos funny – wot I understood of it....I wish e'd fahned a better title. Who's ter know that Pygmalion 'as anyfink to do with a flower girl? 'E mite 'ave called it 'From flower Girl to Duchess'. We should 'ave known wot it was abaht then. Mr Shaw can 'ave this as a tip if 'e likes, free, gratis, and fer nuffink.

The myth

Shaw took the title for his play from the name of Pygmalion (King of Cyprus), a sculptor in Greek mythology. Pygmalion lived in the village of Amathus and was devoted to his statues as he felt they were the only beautiful things around him. He was renowned as a man who disliked all other company, particularly the women of Amathus whose general conduct disgusted him. These women (known as the Propoetides) denied the divinity of Aphrodite (goddess of Love) and so Aphrodite punished them by making them lose all sense of shame so that they gained bad reputations for themselves.

Pygmalion believed in Aphrodite as a goddess and he prayed to her to breathe life into one of his statues. It was an ivory statue which he called Galatea and one he spent a long time making. He fell so much in love with this statue that Aphrodite gave it life. The statue then became a beautiful woman (as created by Pygmalion) and Pygmalion married her.

Historical background

The First World War

Barely four months after *Pygmalion*'s first performance, Britain declared war on Germany. This was the start of the First World War (1914-1918). The events leading up to its outbreak began some time before.

In the Eastern part of Europe (the Balkans) there was a great spread of nationalism in four countries – Greece, Serbia, Montenegro and Bulgaria. The acute problems there led to great unrest culminating in the event said to have sparked the war: the Austrian Archduke (nephew to the reigning Austrian Emperor) and his wife were assassinated by a Serbian student in Sarajevo, the capital city of Bosnia (part of Yugoslavia) on 28 June 1914. One month later in July, Austria declared war on Serbia and the following day Russian forces began to mobilise along the German and Austrian borders. On 1 August Germany declared war on Russia and two days later on France. So many millions of people lost their lives during those four years that the war became known as The Great War – a war to end all wars.

Britain

Shaw's Britain at the time of writing *Pygmalion* in 1912 was alive with new events and achievements. In the so-called Edwardian period (up to the death of Edward VII in 1910) and the few years before the First World War it was thought that 1 per cent of the population owned nearly 70 per cent of the country's wealth – such was the division between what came to be called the upper class and other classes. Shaw's play looks at some of the divisions of this class system in the shape of Eliza, her father, Higgins and his mother.

In the early years of the century the Liberal Government of Prime Minister Asquith attempted to redress some of the balance with the introduction of reforms including school meals, old-age pensions, labour exchanges and National Insurance to help those with less money pay small regular contributions to insure against any future illness. Asquith received much opposition and he found himself facing MPs who did not want such reforms and a country suffering from industrial problems, the difficulties in Ireland from the Home Rule proposals, the suffragette struggles, the mounting European tensions, and the awareness of German re-armament.

Shaw and the Suffragettes

Members of the Women's Social and Political Union (known as Suffragettes) fought to allow women to have the right to vote in the first two decades of the twentieth century. Only in 1918 were women over the age of thirty given the vote and it took until 1928 for women over twenty-one to be enfranchised. The founder of the Union, Mrs Emmeline Pankhurst, had been arrested in 1908, 1909, 1911, 1912 and again in 1913 for what was termed civil disobedience.

Whilst in prison she and many others in favour of women's suffrage went on hunger strike and were often forcibly fed with extremely harmful consequences. In 1913 the Government introduced the Prisoners' Temporary Discharge for Health Act (called the Cat and Mouse Act by those opposed to it) whereby women who refused food in prison could be released on a licence which meant that as soon as they repeated their original offence they would be taken back to prison immediately. As can be imagined this was very unpopular and was criticised by many prominent people, amongst them Shaw:

In the debate on the Dickensian Bill Mr Asquith for the first time opposed the franchise for women explicitly on the grounds that woman is not the female of the human species, but a distinct and inferior species, naturally disqualified from voting as a rabbit is disqualified from voting. It makes it very difficult to vote for the Liberal Party and then look the women of one's household in the face.

This letter to *The Times* written in June 1913 was one example of the way Shaw attacked the Government. Earlier that year he made a speech objecting strongly to the torture of forced feeding:

I contend that this forcible feeding is illegal...I contend that if the Government wants to break people's teeth with chisels, and force food into the lungs and run the risk of killing them, to inflict what is unquestionably torture on them, their business is to bring in a bill legalising these operations. They have no shame in doing it without the law. Why should they be ashamed of doing it with the law?

London theatres

Eliza Doolittle is a flower girl in the Covent Garden area. In 1631 work began here and it was the first part of London to be laid out to a regular plan; the Piazza became the first designed square in the capital. It soon developed into a fashionable meeting place and thoroughfare, and went on to house the largest fruit and vegetable market. Nowadays there is no sign of the old market, which moved to Nine Elms in Vauxhall in 1973. Just as the Southwark area south of the Thames became the birthplace of theatres such as The Rose, The Globe and The Swan in the time of Shakespeare, so the Covent Garden area was used for the building of new theatres after The Restoration from 1660 onwards, following an eighteen-year closure for all theatres during the rule of Cromwell.

The Theatre Royal in Drury Lane was built in 1663 and the first opera house was opened in 1732. His Majesty's Theatre (where *Pygmalion* was first performed) was designed for a wide road to the west of Covent Garden, called The Haymarket. First built in 1705, the present theatre opened in 1899, following fires and complete demolition.

Nowadays this area of what people refer to as London's West End houses more than twenty theatres. Covent Garden's Piazza has been modernised and is now a lively place of shops, restaurants, open-air entertainment and theatre. At 11.15 pm it is just as busy today as it was on that rainy summer evening when Eliza Doolittle met Henry Higgins.

A note on money

In *Pygmalion* there are many references to old British currency which consisted of pounds, shillings and pence – abbreviated to LSD from the Latin names for each: *Librae*, *Solidi* and *Denarii*. This currency was used until 1971 when decimal currency became legal tender. Below is a list of different coins in use for the old money and their equivalent worth in decimal currency.

- *farthing*: $\frac{1}{4}$d, a quarter of an old penny. In 1912 when Shaw wrote the play sweets could be bought for a farthing. No equivalent.

- *halfpenny*: $\frac{1}{2}$d, a half of an old penny, referred to as ha' penny. No equivalent.

- *penny*: 1d, the coin was called a penny but anything above one penny was referred to as pence, e.g. 2d = two-pence, pronounced 'tuppence'. Equivalent of $\frac{1}{2}$ new pence.

- *threepenny-piece*: 3d, pronounced 'thrupence'. Equivalent of between 1 and $1\frac{1}{2}$ new pence.

- *sixpenny-piece*: 6d, sixpence, in slang called a 'tanner'. Equivalent of $2\frac{1}{2}$ p.

- *shilling*: 1s, written as 1/-, in slang called a 'bob'. Equivalent of 5p.

- *two-shilling-piece*: 2/-, also called a florin. Equivalent of 10p.

- *half-a-crown*: 2/6d; quite a large coin. Equivalent of $12\frac{1}{2}$ p.

There were 12 pennies in a shilling; 20 shillings in a pound; 240 pennies in a pound. Pound coins were called 'sovereigns'. There were also pound notes, and a ten-shilling note instead of the 50p piece.

To give an idea of just how much the cost of living has changed, in the programme for the first performance of *Pygmalion* someone going to a matinee performance could have tea, bread and butter and cakes all for sixpence, the equivalent of $2\frac{1}{2}$ p! Nowadays, in the 1990s, this could cost well over £2.50.

Reading log

One of the easiest ways of keeping track of your reading is to keep a log book. This can be any exercise book or folder that you have to hand, but make sure you reserve it exclusively for reflecting on your reading, both at home and in school.

As you read the play, stop from time to time and think back over what you have read.

- Is there anything that puzzles you? Note down some questions that you might want to research, discuss with your friends, or ask a teacher. Also note any quotations which strike you as important or memorable.

- Does your reading remind you of anything else you have read, heard or seen on TV or at the cinema? Jot down what it is and where the similarities lie.

- Have you had any similar experiences to those occurring in the play? Do you find yourself identifying closely with one or more of the characters? Record this as accurately as you can.

- Do you find yourself really liking, or really loathing, any of the characters? What is it about them that makes you feel so strongly? Make notes that you can add to.

- Can you picture the locations and settings? Draw maps, plans, diagrams, drawings, in fact any doodle that helps you make sense of these things.

- Now and again try to predict what will happen next in the play. Use what you already know of the author and the characters to help you do this. Later record how close you were and whether you are surprised at the outcome.

- Write down any feelings that you have about the play. Your reading log should help you make sense of your own ideas alongside those of the author.

Pygmalion

NOTE FOR TECHNICIANS. A complete representation of the play as printed in this edition is technically possible only on the cinema screen or on stages furnished with exceptionally elaborate machinery. For ordinary theatrical use the scenes separated by rows of asterisks are to be omitted.

In the dialogue an e upside down indicates the indefinite vowel, sometimes called obscure or neutral, for which, though it is one of the commonest sounds in English speech, our wretched alphabet has no letter.

PREFACE TO *PYGMALION*

A Professor of Phonetics

As will be seen later on, Pygmalion needs, not a preface, but a sequel, which I have supplied in its due place.

The English have no respect for their language, and will not teach their children to speak it. They cannot spell it because they have nothing to spell it with but an old foreign alphabet of which only the consonants—and not all of them—have any agreed speech value. Consequently no man can teach himself what it should sound like from reading it; and it is impossible for an Englishman to open his mouth without making some other Englishman despise him. Most European languages are now accessible in black and white to foreigners: English and French are not thus accessible even to Englishmen and Frenchmen. The reformer we need most today is an energetic phonetic enthusiast: that is why I have made such a one the hero of a popular play.

There have been heroes of that kind crying in the wilderness for many years past. When I became interested in the subject towards the end of the eighteen-seventies, the illustrious Alexander Melville Bell, the inventor of Visible Speech, had emigrated to Canada, where his son invented the telephone; but Alexander J. Ellis was still a London patriarch, with an impressive head always covered by a velvet skull cap, for which he would apologize to public meetings in a very courtly manner. He and Tito Pagliardini, another phonetic veteran, were men whom it was impossible to dislike. Henry Sweet, then a young man, lacked their sweetness of character: he was about as conciliatory to conventional mortals as Ibsen or Samuel Butler. His great ability as a phonetician (he was, I think, the best of them all at his job) would have entitled him to high official recognition, and perhaps enabled him to popularize his subject, but for his Satanic contempt for all academic dignitaries and persons in general who thought more of Greek than of phonetics. Once, in the days when the Imperial Institute rose in South Kensington, and Joseph Chamberlain was booming the Empire, I induced the editor of a leading monthly review to commission an article from Sweet on the imperial importance of his subject. When it arrived, it contained nothing but a savagely derisive attack on a professor of language and literature whose chair Sweet regarded as proper to a phonetic expert only. The article, being libellous, had to be returned as impossible; and I had to renounce my dream of dragging its author into the limelight. When I met him afterwards, for the first time for many years, I found to my astonishment that he, who had been a quite tolerably presentable young man, had actually managed by sheer scorn to alter his personal appearance until he had become a sort of walking repudiation of Oxford and all its traditions. It must have been largely in his own despite that he was squeezed into something called a Readership of phonetics there. The future of phonetics rests probably with his pupils, who all swore by him; but nothing could bring the man himself into any sort of compliance with the university to which he nevertheless clung by divine right in an intensely Oxonian way. I daresay his papers, if he has left any, include some satires that may be published without too destructive results fifty years hence. He was, I believe, not in the least an illnatured man: very much the opposite, I should say; but he would not suffer fools gladly; and to him all scholars who were not rabid phoneticians were fools.

Those who knew him will recognize in my third act the allusion to the Current Shorthand in which he used to write postcards. It may be acquired from a four and sixpenny manual published by the Clarendon Press. The postcards which Mrs Higgins describes are such as I have received from Sweet. I would decipher a sound which a cockney would represent by ʒerr, and a Frenchman by seu, and then write demanding with some heat what on earth it meant. Sweet, with boundless contempt for my stupidity, would reply that it not only meant but obviously was the word Result, as no other word containing that sound, and capable of making sense with the context, existed in any language spoken on earth. That less expert mortals should require fuller indications was beyond Sweet's patience. Therefore, though the whole point of his Current Shorthand is that it can express every sound in the language perfectly, vowels as well as consonants, and that your hand has to make no stroke except the easy and current ones with which you write m, n, and u, l, p, and q, scribbling them at whatever angle comes easiest to you, his unfortunate determination to make this remarkable and quite legible script serve also as a shorthand reduced it in his own practice to the most inscrutable of cryptograms. His true objective was the provision of a full, accurate, legible script for our language; but he was led past that by his contempt for the popular Pitman system of shorthand, which he called the Pitfall system. The triumph of Pitman was a triumph of business organization: there was a weekly paper to persuade you to learn Pitman: there were cheap textbooks and exercise books and transcripts of speeches for you to copy, and schools where experienced teachers coached you up to the necessary proficiency. Sweet could not organize his market in that fashion. He might as well have been the Sybil who tore up the leaves of prophecy that nobody would attend to. The four and sixpenny manual, mostly in his lithographed handwriting, that was never vulgarly advertized, may perhaps some day be taken up by a syndicate and pushed upon the public as The Times pushed the Encyclopædia Britannica; but until then it will certainly not prevail against Pitman. I have bought three copies of it during my lifetime; and I am informed by the publishers that its cloistered existence is still a steady and healthy one. I actually learned the system two several times; and yet the shorthand in which I am writing these lines is Pitman's. And the reason is, that my secretary cannot transcribe Sweet, having been perforce taught in the schools of Pitman. In America I could use the commercially organized Gregg shorthand, which has taken a hint from Sweet by making its letters writable (current, Sweet would have called them) instead of having to be geometrically drawn like Pitman's; but all these systems, including Sweet's, are spoilt by making them available for verbatim reporting, in which complete and exact spelling and word division are impossible. A complete and exact phonetic script is neither practicable nor necessary for ordinary use; but if we enlarge our alphabet to the Russian size, and make our spelling as phonetic as Spanish, the advance will be prodigious.

Pygmalion Higgins is not a portrait of Sweet, to whom the adventure of Eliza Doolittle would have been impossible; still, as will be seen, there are touches of Sweet in the play. With Higgins's physique and temperament Sweet might have set the Thames on fire. As it was, he impressed himself professionally on Europe to an extent that made his comparative personal obscurity, and the failure of Oxford to do justice to his eminence, a puzzle to foreign specialists in his subject. I do not blame Oxford, because I think Oxford is quite right in demanding a certain social amenity from its nurslings (heaven knows it is not exorbitant in its requirements!); for although I well know how hard it is for a man of genius with a seriously underrated subject to maintain serene and kindly relations with the men who underrate it, and who keep all the best places for less important subjects which they profess without originality and sometimes without much capacity for them, still, if he overwhelms them with wrath and disdain, he cannot expect them to heap honors on him.

Of the later generations of phoneticians I know little. Among them towered Robert Bridges, to whom perhaps Higgins may owe his Miltonic sympathies, though here again I must disclaim all portraiture. But if the play makes the public aware that there are such people as phoneticians, and that they are among the most important people in England at present, it will serve its turn.

I wish to boast that Pygmalion has been an extremely successful play, both on stage and screen, all over Europe and North

PREFACE

America as well as at home. It is so intensely and deliberately didactic, and its subject is esteemed so dry, that I delight in throwing it at the heads of the wiseacres who repeat the parrot cry that art should never be didactic. It goes to prove my contention that great art can never be anything else.

Finally, and for the encouragement of people troubled with accents that cut them off from all high employment, I may add that the change wrought by Professor Higgins in the flower-girl is neither impossible nor uncommon. The modern concierge's daughter who fulfils her ambition by playing the Queen of Spain in Ruy Blas at the Theatre Francais is only one of many thousands of men and women who have sloughed off their native dialects and acquired a new tongue. Our West End shop assistants and domestic servants are bi-lingual. But the thing has to be done scientifically, or the last state of the aspirant may be worse than the first. An honest slum dialect is more tolerable than the attempts of phonetically untaught persons to imitate the plutocracy. Ambitious flower-girls who read this play must not imagine that they can pass themselves off as fine ladies by untutored imitation. They must learn their alphabet over again, and different, from a phonetic expert. Imitation will only make them ridiculous.

CHARACTERS

in the order of their appearance

THE DAUGHTER /CLARA EYNSFORD HILL
THE MOTHER /MRS EYNSFORD HILL
A BYSTANDER
FREDDY EYNSFORD HILL
THE FLOWER GIRL /ELIZA DOOLITTLE
THE GENTLEMAN /COLONEL PICKERING
THE NOTE TAKER /PROFESSOR HENRY HIGGINS
BYSTANDERS
SARCASTIC BYSTANDER
TAXIMAN
MRS PEARCE
ALFRED DOOLITTLE
MRS HIGGINS
THE PARLOR-MAID
WHISKERS /NEPOMMUCK
FOOTMAN
FIRST LANDING FOOTMAN
SECOND LANDING FOOTMAN
HOSTESS
HOST
CONSTABLE
SECOND CONSTABLE

6

ACT I

London at 11.15 p.m. Torrents of heavy summer rain. Cab whistles blowing frantically in all directions. Pedestrians running for shelter into the portico of St Paul's church (not Wren's cathedral but Inigo Jones's church in Covent Garden vegetable market), among them a lady and her daughter in evening dress. All are peering out gloomily at the rain, except one man with his back turned to the rest, wholly preoccupied with a notebook in which he is writing.

The church clock strikes the first quarter.

THE DAUGHTER [*in the space between the central pillars, close to the one on her left*] I'm getting chilled to the bone. What can Freddy be doing all this time? He's been gone twenty minutes.

THE MOTHER [*on her daughter's right*] Not so long. But he ought to have got us a cab by this.

A BYSTANDER [*on the lady's right*] He wont get no cab not until half-past eleven, missus, when they come back after dropping their theatre fares.

THE MOTHER. But we must have a cab. We cant stand here until half-past eleven. It's too bad.

THE BYSTANDER. Well, it aint my fault, missus.

THE DAUGHTER. If Freddy had a bit of gumption, he would have got one at the theatre door.

THE MOTHER. What could he have done, poor boy?

THE DAUGHTER. Other people got cabs. Why couldnt he?

Freddy rushes in out of the rain from the Southampton Street side, and comes between them closing a dripping umbrella. He is a young man of twenty, in evening dress, very wet round the ankles.

THE DAUGHTER. Well, havnt you got a cab?

FREDDY. Theres not one to be had for love or money.

THE MOTHER. Oh, Freddy, there must be one. You cant have tried.

7

THE DAUGHTER. It's too tiresome. Do you expect us to go and get one ourselves?

FREDDY. I tell you theyre all engaged. The rain was so sudden: nobody was prepared; and everybody had to take a cab. Ive been to Charing Cross one way and nearly to Ludgate Circus the other; and they were all engaged.

THE MOTHER. Did you try Trafalgar Square?

FREDDY. There wasnt one at Trafalgar Square.

THE DAUGHTER. Did you try?

FREDDY. I tried as far as Charing Cross Station. Did you expect me to walk to Hammersmith?

THE DAUGHTER. You havnt tried at all.

THE MOTHER. You really are very helpless, Freddy. Go again; and dont come back until you have found a cab.

FREDDY. I shall simply get soaked for nothing.

THE DAUGHTER. And what about us? Are we to stay here all night in this draught, with next to nothing on? You selfish pig—

FREDDY. Oh, very well: I'll go, I'll go. [*He opens his umbrella and dashes off Strandwards, but comes into collision with a flower girl who is hurrying in for shelter, knocking her basket out of her hands. A blinding flash of lightning, followed instantly by a rattling peal of thunder, orchestrates the incident*].

THE FLOWER GIRL. Nah then, Freddy: look wh' y' gowin, deah.

FREDDY. Sorry [*he rushes off*].

THE FLOWER GIRL [*picking up her scattered flowers and replacing them in the basket*] Theres menners f' yer! Tǝ-oo banches o voylets trod into the mad. [*She sits down on the plinth of the column, sorting her flowers, on the lady's right. She is not at all a romantic figure. She is perhaps eighteen, perhaps twenty, hardly older. She wears a little sailor hat of black straw that has long been exposed to the dust and soot of London and has seldom if ever been brushed. Her hair needs washing rather badly: its mousy color can hardly be natural. She wears a shoddy black coat that reaches nearly to her knees and is shaped to her waist. She has a brown skirt with a coarse apron. Her boots are much the worse for wear. She is no doubt as clean as she can afford to be; but compared to the ladies she is very dirty. Her features are no worse than theirs; but their condition leaves something to be desired; and she needs the services of a dentist].*

THE MOTHER. How do you know that my son's name is Freddy, pray?

THE FLOWER GIRL. Ow, eez yə-ooa san, is e? Wal, fewd dan y' də-ooty bawmz a mather should, eed now bettern to spawl a pore gel's flahrzn then ran awy athaht pyin. Will yə-oo py me f'them? [*Here, with apologies, this desperate attempt to represent her dialect without a phonetic alphabet must be abandoned as unintelligible outside London*].

THE DAUGHTER. Do nothing of the sort, mother. The idea!

THE MOTHER. Please allow me, Clara. Have you any pennies?

THE DAUGHTER. No. Ive nothing smaller than sixpence.

THE FLOWER GIRL [*hopefully*] I can give you change for a tanner, kind lady.

THE MOTHER [*to Clara*] Give it to me. [*Clara parts reluctantly*]. Now [*to the girl*] This is for your flowers.

THE FLOWER GIRL. Thank you kindly, lady.

THE DAUGHTER. Make her give you the change. These things are only a penny a bunch.

THE MOTHER. Do hold your tongue, Clara. [*To the girl*] You can keep the change.

THE FLOWER GIRL. Oh, thank you, lady.

THE MOTHER. Now tell me how you know that young gentleman's name.

THE FLOWER GIRL. I didnt.

THE MOTHER. I heard you call him by it. Dont try to deceive me.

THE FLOWER GIRL [*protesting*] Who's trying to deceive you? I called him Freddy or Charlie same as you might yourself if you was talking to a stranger and wished to be pleasant.

THE DAUGHTER. Sixpence thrown away! Really, mamma, you

9

might have spared Freddy that. [*She retreats in disgust behind the pillar*].

An elderly gentleman of the amiable military type rushes into the shelter, and closes a dripping umbrella. He is in the same plight as Freddy, very wet about the ankles. He is in evening dress, with a light overcoat. He takes the place left vacant by the daughter.

THE GENTLEMAN. Phew!

THE MOTHER [*to the gentleman*] Oh, sir, is there any sign of its stopping?

THE GENTLEMAN. I'm afraid not. It started worse than ever about two minutes ago [*he goes to the plinth beside the flower girl; puts up his foot on it; and stoops to turn down his trouser ends*].

THE MOTHER. Oh dear! [*She retires sadly and joins her daughter*].

THE FLOWER GIRL [*taking advantage of the military gentleman's proximity to establish friendly relations with him*] If it's worse, it's a sign it's nearly over. So cheer up, Captain; and buy a flower off a poor girl.

THE GENTLEMAN. I'm sorry. I havnt any change.

THE FLOWER GIRL. I can give you change, Captain.

THE GENTLEMAN. For a sovereign? Ive nothing less.

THE FLOWER GIRL. Garn! Oh do buy a flower off me, Captain. I can change half-a-crown. Take this for tuppence.

THE GENTLEMAN. Now dont be troublesome: theres a good girl. [*Trying his pockets*] I really havnt any change—Stop: heres three hapence, if thats any use to you [*he retreats to the other pillar*].

THE FLOWER GIRL [*disappointed, but thinking three halfpence better than nothing*] Thank you, sir.

THE BYSTANDER [*to the girl*] You be careful: give him a flower for it. Theres a bloke here behind taking down every blessed word youre saying. [*All turn to the man who is taking notes*].

THE FLOWER GIRL [*springing up terrified*] I aint done nothing wrong by speaking to the gentleman. Ive a right to sell flowers if I keep off the kerb. [*Hysterically*] I'm a respectable girl: so help me, I never spoke to him except to ask him to buy a flower off me.

General hubbub, mostly sympathetic to the flower girl, but deprecating her excessive sensibility. Cries of Dont start hollerin. Who's hurting you? Nobody's going to touch you. Whats the good of fussing? Steady on. Easy easy, *etc., come from the elderly staid spectators, who pat her comfortingly. Less patient ones bid her shut her head, or ask her roughly what is wrong with her. A remoter group, not knowing what the matter is, crowd in and increase the noise with question and answer:* Whats the row? What-she do? Where is he? A tec taking her down. What! him? Yes: him over there: Took money off the gentleman, *etc.*

THE FLOWER GIRL [*breaking through them to the gentleman, crying wildly*] Oh, sir, dont let him charge me. You dunno what it means to me. Theyll take away my character and drive me on the streets for speaking to gentlemen. They—

THE NOTE TAKER [*coming forward on her right, the rest crowding after him*] There! there! there! there! who's hurting you, you silly girl? What do you take me for?

THE BYSTANDER. It's aw rawt: e's a genleman: look at his bə-oots. [*Explaining to the note taker*] She thought you was a copper's nark, sir.

THE NOTE TAKER [*with quick interest*] Whats a copper's nark?

THE BYSTANDER [*inapt at definition*] It's a—well, it's a copper's nark, as you might say. What else would you call it? A sort of informer.

THE FLOWER GIRL [*still hysterical*] I take my Bible oath I never said a word—

THE NOTE TAKER [*overbearing but good-humored*] Oh, shut up, shut up. Do I look like a policeman?

THE FLOWER GIRL [*far from reassured*] Then what did you take down my words for? How do I know whether you took me down right? You just shew me what youve wrote about me. [*The note taker opens his book and holds it steadily under her nose, though the pressure of the mob trying to read it over his shoulders would upset a weaker man*]. Whats that? That aint proper writing. I cant read that.

THE NOTE TAKER. I can. [*Reads, reproducing her pronunciation exactly*] "Cheer ap, Keptin; n' baw ya flahr orf a pore gel."

THE FLOWER GIRL [*much distressed*] It's because I called him Captain. I meant no harm. [*To the gentleman*] Oh, sir, dont let him lay a charge agen me for a word like that. You—

THE GENTLEMAN. Charge! I make no charge. [*To the note taker*] Really, sir, if you are a detective, you need not begin protecting me against molestation by young women until I ask you. Anybody could see that the girl meant no harm.

THE BYSTANDERS GENERALLY [*demonstrating against police espionage*] Course they could. What business is it of yours? You mind your own affairs. He wants promotion, he does. Taking down people's words! Girl never said a word to him. What harm if she did? Nice thing a girl cant shelter from the rain without being insulted, etc., etc., etc. [*She is conducted by the more sympathetic demonstrators back to her plinth, where she resumes her seat and struggles with her emotion*].

THE BYSTANDER. He aint a tec. He's a blooming busybody: thats what he is. I tell you, look at his bə-oots.

THE NOTE TAKER [*turning on him genially*] And how are all your people down at Selsey?

THE BYSTANDER [*suspiciously*] Who told you my people come from Selsey?

THE NOTE TAKER. Never you mind. They did. [*To the girl*] How do you come to be up so far east? You were born in Lisson Grove.

THE FLOWER GIRL [*appalled*] Oh, what harm is there in my leaving Lisson Grove? It wasnt fit for a pig to live in; and I had to pay four-and-six a week. [*In tears*] Oh, boo—hoo—oo—

THE NOTE TAKER. Live where you like; but stop that noise.

THE GENTLEMAN [*to the girl*] Come, come! he cant touch you: you have a right to live where you please.

A SARCASTIC BYSTANDER [*thrusting himself between the note taker and the gentleman*] Park Lane, for instance. I'd like to go into the

Housing Question with you, I would.

THE FLOWER GIRL [*subsiding into a brooding melancholy over her basket, and talking very low-spiritedly to herself*] I'm a good girl, I am.

THE SARCASTIC BYSTANDER [*not attending to her*] Do you know where *I* come from?

THE NOTE TAKER [*promptly*] Hoxton.

Titterings. Popular interest in the note taker's performance increases.

THE SARCASTIC ONE [*amazed*] Well, who said I didnt? Bly me! you know everything, you do.

THE FLOWER GIRL [*still nursing her sense of injury*] Aint no call to meddle with me, he aint.

THE BYSTANDER [*to her*] Of course he aint. Dont you stand it from him. [*To the note taker*] See here: what call have you to know about people what never offered to meddle with you?

THE FLOWER GIRL. Let him say what he likes. I dont want to have no truck with him.

THE BYSTANDER. You take us for dirt under your feet, dont you? Catch you taking liberties with a gentleman!

THE SARCASTIC BYSTANDER. Yes: tell him where he come from if you want to go fortune-telling.

THE NOTE TAKER. Cheltenham, Harrow, Cambridge, and India.

THE GENTLEMAN. Quite right.

Great laughter. Reaction in the note taker's favor. Exclamations of He knows all about it. Told him proper. Hear him tell the toff where he come from? *etc.*

THE GENTLEMAN. May I ask, sir, do you do this for your living at a music hall?

THE NOTE TAKER. I've thought of that. Perhaps I shall some day.

The rain has stopped; and the persons on the outside of the crowd begin to drop off.

THE FLOWER GIRL [*resenting the reaction*] He's no gentleman, he aint, to interfere with a poor girl.

THE DAUGHTER [*out of patience, pushing her way rudely to the front and displacing the gentleman, who politely retires to the other side of the pillar*] What on earth is Freddy doing? I shall get pneumownia if I stay in this draught any longer.

THE NOTE TAKER [*to himself, hastily making a note of her pronunciation of "monia"*] Earlscourt.

THE DAUGHTER [*violently*] Will you please keep your impertinent remarks to yourself.

THE NOTE TAKER. Did I say that out loud? I didnt mean to. I beg your pardon. Your mother's Epsom, unmistakeably.

THE MOTHER [*advancing between her daughter and the note taker*] How very curious! I was brought up in Largelady Park, near Epsom.

THE NOTE TAKER [*uproariously amused*] Ha! ha! What a devil of a name! Excuse me. [*To the daughter*] You want a cab, do you?

THE DAUGHTER. Dont dare speak to me.

THE MOTHER. Oh please, please, Clara. [*Her daughter repudiates her with an angry shrug and retires haughtily*]. We should be so grateful to you, sir, if you found us a cab. [*The note taker produces a whistle*]. Oh, thank you. [*She joins her daughter*].

The note taker blows a piercing blast.

THE SARCASTIC BYSTANDER. There! I knowed he was a plainclothes copper.

THE BYSTANDER. That aint a police whistle: thats a sporting whistle.

THE FLOWER GIRL [*still preoccupied with her wounded feelings*] He's no right to take away my character. My character is the same to me as any lady's.

THE NOTE TAKER. I dont know whether youve noticed it; but the rain stopped about two minutes ago.

THE BYSTANDER. So it has. Why didnt you say so before? and us losing our time listening to your silliness! [*He walks off towards the Strand*].

THE SARCASTIC BYSTANDER. I can tell where you come from. You come from Anwell. Go back there.

THE NOTE TAKER [*helpfully*] *H*anwell.

THE SARCASTIC BYSTANDER [*affecting great distinction of speech*] Thenk you, teacher. Haw haw! So long [*he touches his hat with mock respect and strolls off*].

THE FLOWER GIRL. Frightening people like that! How would he like it himself?

THE MOTHER. It's quite fine now, Clara. We can walk to a motor bus. Come. [*She gathers her skirts above her ankles and hurries off towards the Strand*].

THE DAUGHTER. But the cab—[*her mother is out of hearing*]. Oh, how tiresome! [*She follows angrily*].

All the rest have gone except the note taker, the gentleman, and the flower girl, who sits arranging her basket, and still pitying herself in murmurs.

THE FLOWER GIRL. Poor girl! Hard enough for her to live without being worrited and chivied.

THE GENTLEMAN [*returning to his former place on the note taker's left*] How do you do it, if I may ask?

THE NOTE TAKER. Simply phonetics. The science of speech. Thats my profession: also my hobby. Happy is the man who can make a living by his hobby! You can spot an Irishman or a Yorkshireman by his brogue. *I* can place any man within six miles. I can place him within two miles in London. Sometimes within two streets.

THE FLOWER GIRL. Ought to be ashamed of himself, unmanly coward!

THE GENTLEMAN. But is there a living in that?

THE NOTE TAKER. Oh yes. Quite a fat one. This is an age of upstarts. Men begin in Kentish Town with £80 a year, and end in Park Lane with a hundred thousand. They want to drop Kentish Town; but they give themselves away every time they open their mouths. Now I can teach them—

15

THE FLOWER GIRL. Let him mind his own business and leave a poor girl—

THE NOTE TAKER [*explosively*] Woman: cease this detestable boohooing instantly; or else seek the shelter of some other place of worship.

THE FLOWER GIRL [*with feeble defiance*] Ive a right to be here if I like, same as you.

THE NOTE TAKER. A woman who utters such depressing and disgusting sounds has no right to be anywhere—no right to live. Remember that you are a human being with a soul and the divine gift of articulate speech: that your native language is the language of Shakespear and Milton and The Bible; and dont sit there crooning like a bilious pigeon.

THE FLOWER GIRL [*quite overwhelmed, looking up at him in mingled wonder and deprecation without daring to raise her head*] Ah-ah-ah-ow-ow-ow-oo!

THE NOTE TAKER [*whipping out his book*] Heavens! what a sound! [*He writes; then holds out the book and reads, reproducing her vowels exactly*] Ah-ah-ah-ow-ow-ow-oo!

THE FLOWER GIRL [*tickled by the performance, and laughing in spite of herself*] Garn!

THE NOTE TAKER. You see this creature with her kerbstone English: the English that will keep her in the gutter to the end of her days. Well, sir, in three months I could pass that girl off as a duchess at an ambassador's garden party. I could even get her a place as lady's maid or shop assistant, which requires better English.

THE FLOWER GIRL. What's that you say?

THE NOTE TAKER. Yes, you squashed cabbage leaf, you disgrace to the noble architecture of these columns, you incarnate insult to the English language: I could pass you off as the Queen of Sheba. [*To the Gentleman*] Can you believe that?

THE GENTLEMAN. Of course I can. I am myself a student of Indian dialects; and—

THE NOTE TAKER [*eagerly*] Are you? Do you know Colonel Pickering, the author of Spoken Sanscrit?

THE GENTLEMAN. I am Colonel Pickering. Who are you?

THE NOTE TAKER. Henry Higgins, author of Higgins's Universal Alphabet.

PICKERING [*with enthusiasm*] I came from India to meet you.

HIGGINS. I was going to India to meet you.

PICKERING. Where do you live?

HIGGINS. 27A Wimpole Street. Come and see me tomorrow.

PICKERING. I'm at the Carlton. Come with me now and lets have a jaw over some supper.

HIGGINS. Right you are.

THE FLOWER GIRL [*to Pickering, as he passes her*] Buy a flower, kind gentleman. I'm short for my lodging.

PICKERING. I really havnt any change. I'm sorry [*he goes away*].

HIGGINS [*shocked at the girl's mendacity*] Liar. You said you could change half-a-crown.

THE FLOWER GIRL [*rising in desperation*] You ought to be stuffed with nails, you ought. [*Flinging the basket at his feet*] Take the whole blooming basket for sixpence.

The church clock strikes the second quarter.

HIGGINS [*hearing in it the voice of God, rebuking him for his Pharisaic want of charity to the poor girl*] A reminder. [*He raises his hat solemnly; then throws a handful of money into the basket and follows Pickering*].

THE FLOWER GIRL [*picking up a half-crown*] Ah-ow-ooh! [*Picking up a couple of florins*] Aaah-ow-ooh! [*Picking up several coins*] Aaaaaah-ow-ooh! [*Picking up a half-sovereign*] Aaaaaaaaaaaah-ow-ooh!!!

FREDDY [*springing out of a taxicab*] Got one at last. Hallo! [*To the girl*] Where are the two ladies that were here?

THE FLOWER GIRL. They walked to the bus when the rain stopped.

FREDDY. And left me with a cab on my hands! Damnation!

PYGMALION

THE FLOWER GIRL [*with grandeur*] Never mind, young man. I'm going home in a taxi. [*She sails off to the cab. The driver puts his hand behind him and holds the door firmly shut against her. Quite understanding his mistrust, she shews him her handful of money*]. A taxi fare aint to object to me, Charlie. [*He grins and opens the door*]. Here. What about the basket?

THE TAXIMAN. Give it here. Tuppence extra.

THE FLOWER GIRL. No: I dont want nobody to see it. [*She crushes it into the cab and gets in, continuing the conversation through the window*] Goodbye, Freedy.

FREDDY [*dazedly raising his hat*] Goodbye.

TAXIMAN. Where to?

THE FLOWER GIRL. Bucknam Pellis [Buckingham Palace].

TAXIMAN. What d'ye mean—Bucknam Pellis?

THE FLOWER GIRL. Dont you know where it is? In the Green Park, where the King lives. Goodbye, Freedy. Dont let me keep you standing there. Goodbye.

FREDDY. Goodbye. [*He goes*].

TAXIMAN. Here? Whats this about Bucknam Pellis? What business have you at Bucknam Pellis?

THE FLOWER GIRL. Of course I havnt none. But I wasnt going to let him know that. You drive me home.

TAXIMAN. And wheres home?

THE FLOWER GIRL. Angel Court, Drury Lane, next Meiklejohn's oil shop.

TAXIMAN. That sounds more like it, Judy. [*He drives off*].

* * * * * *

Let us follow the taxi to the entrance to Angel Court, a narrow little archway between two shops, one of them Meiklejohn's oil shop. When it stops there, Eliza gets out, dragging her basket with her.

THE FLOWER GIRL. How much?

TAXIMAN [*indicating the taximeter*] Cant you read? A shilling.

THE FLOWER GIRL. A shilling for two minutes!!

TAXIMAN. Two minutes or ten: it's all the same.

PYGMALION

THE FLOWER GIRL. Well, I dont call it right.

TAXIMAN. Ever been in a taxi before?

THE FLOWER GIRL [*with dignity*] Hundreds and thousands of times, young man.

TAXIMAN [*laughing at her*] Good for you, Judy. Keep the shilling, darling, with best love from all at home. Good luck! [*He drives off*].

THE FLOWER GIRL [*humiliated*] Impidence!

She picks up the basket and trudges up the alley with it to her lodging: a small room with very old wall paper hanging loose in the damp places. A broken pane in the window is mended with paper. A portrait of a popular actor and a fashion plate of ladies' dresses, all wildly beyond the poor flower girl's means, both torn from newspapers, are pinned up on the wall. A birdcage hangs in the window; but its tenant died long ago: it remains as a memorial only.

These are the only visible luxuries: the rest is the irreducible minimum of poverty's needs: a wretched bed heaped with all sorts of coverings that have any warmth in them, a draped packing case with a basin and jug on it and a little looking glass over it, a chair and table, the refuse of some suburban kitchen, and an American alarum clock on the shelf above the unused fireplace: the whole lighted with a gas lamp with a penny in the slot meter. Rent: four shillings a week.

Here the flower girl, chronically weary, but too excited to go to bed, sits, counting her new riches and dreaming and planning what to do with them, until the gas goes out, when she enjoys for the first time the sensation of being able to put in another penny without grudging it. This prodigal mood does not extinguish her gnawing sense of the need for economy sufficiently to prevent her from calculating that she can dream and plan in bed more cheaply and warmly than sitting up without a fire. So she takes off her shawl and skirt and adds them to the miscellaneous bed-clothes. Then she kicks off her shoes and gets into bed without any further change.

ACT II

Next day at 11 a.m. Higgins's laboratory in Wimpole Street. It is a room on the first floor, looking on the street, and was meant for the drawing room. The double doors are in the middle of the back wall; and persons entering find in the corner to their right two tall file cabinets at right angles to one another against the walls. In this corner stands a flat writing-table, on which are a phonograph, a laryngoscope, a row of tiny organ pipes with a bellows, a set of lamp chimneys for singing flames with burners attached to a gas plug in the wall by an indiarubber tube, several tuning-forks of different sizes, a life-size image of half a human head, shewing in section the vocal organs, and a box containing a supply of wax cylinders for the phonograph.

Further down the room, on the same side, is a fireplace, with a comfortable leather-covered easy-chair at the side of the hearth nearest the door, and a coal-scuttle. There is a clock on the mantelpiece. Between the fireplace and the phonograph table is a stand for newspapers.

On the other side of the central door, to the left of the visitor, is a cabinet of shallow drawers. On it is a telephone and the telephone directory. The corner beyond, and most of the side wall, is occupied by a grand piano, with the keyboard at the end furthest from the door, and a bench for the player extending the full length of the keyboard. On the piano is a dessert dish heaped with fruit and sweets, mostly chocolates.

The middle of the room is clear. Besides the easy-chair, the piano bench, and two chairs at the phonograph table, there is one stray chair. It stands near the fireplace. On the walls, engravings: mostly Piranesi and mezzotint portraits. No paintings.

Pickering is seated at the table, putting down some cards and a tuning-fork which he has been using. Higgins is standing up near him, closing two or three file drawers which are hanging out. He appears in the morning light as a robust, vital, appetizing sort of

PYGMALION

man of forty or thereabouts, dressed in a professional-looking black frock-coat with a white linen collar and black silk tie. He is of the energetic, scientific type, heartily, even violently interested in every-thing that can be studied as a scientific subject, and careless about himself and other people, including their feelings. He is, in fact, but for his years and size, rather like a very impetuous baby "taking notice" eagerly and loudly, and requiring almost as much watching to keep him out of unintended mischief. His manner varies from genial bullying when he is in a good humor to stormy petulance when anything goes wrong; but he is so entirely frank and void of malice that he remains likeable even in his least reasonable moments.

HIGGINS [*as he shuts the last drawer*] Well, I think thats the whole show.

PICKERING. It's really amazing. I havnt taken half of it in, you know.

HIGGINS. Would you like to go over any of it again?

PICKERING [*rising and coming to the fireplace, where he plants himself with his back to the fire*] No, thank you: not now. I'm quite done up for this morning.

HIGGINS [*following him, and standing beside him on his left*] Tired of listening to sounds?

PICKERING. Yes. It's a fearful strain. I rather fancied myself because I can pronounce twenty-four distinct vowel sounds; but your hundred and thirty beat me. I cant hear a bit of difference between most of them.

HIGGINS [*chuckling, and going over to the piano to eat sweets*] Oh, that comes with practice. You hear no difference at first; but you keep on listening, and presently you find theyre all as different as A from B. [*Mrs Pearce looks in: she is Higgins's housekeeper*]. Whats the matter?

MRS PEARCE [*hesitating, evidently perplexed*] A young woman asks to see you, sir.

HIGGINS. A young woman! What does she want?

MRS PEARCE. Well, sir, she says youll be glad to see her when you know what she's come about. She's quite a common girl, sir. Very common indeed. I should have sent her away, only I thought perhaps you wanted her to talk into your machines. I hope Ive not done wrong; but really you see such queer people sometimes— youll excuse me, I'm sure, sir—

HIGGINS. Oh, thats all right, Mrs Pearce. Has she an interesting accent?

MRS PEARCE. Oh, something dreadful, sir, really. I dont know how you can take an interest in it.

HIGGINS [to Pickering] Lets have her up. Shew her up, Mrs Pearce [he rushes across to his working table and picks out a cylinder to use on the phonograph].

MRS PEARCE [only half resigned to it] Very well, sir. It's for you to say. [She goes downstairs].

HIGGINS. This is rather a bit of luck. I'll shew you how I make records. We'll set her talking; and I'll take it down first in Bell's visible Speech; then in broad Romic; and then we'll get her on the phonograph so that you can turn her on as often as you like with the written transcript before you.

MRS PEARCE [returning] This is the young woman, sir.

The flower girl enters in state. She has a hat with three ostrich feathers, orange, sky-blue, and red. She has a nearly clean apron, and the shoddy coat has been tidied a little. The pathos of this deplorable figure, with its innocent vanity and consequential air, touches Pickering, who has already straightened himself in the presence of Mrs Pearce. But as to Higgins, the only distinction he makes between men and women is that when he is neither bullying nor exclaiming to the heavens against some feather-weight cross, he coaxes women as a child coaxes its nurse when it wants to get anything out of her.

HIGGINS [brusquely, recognizing her with unconcealed disappointment, and at once, babylike, making an intolerable grievance of it] Why, this is the girl I jotted down last night. She's no use: Ive got all the records I want of the Lisson Grove lingo; and I'm not going to waste another cylinder on it. [*To the girl*] Be off with you: I dont want you.

THE FLOWER GIRL. Dont you be so saucy. You aint heard what I come for yet. [*To Mrs Pearce, who is waiting at the door for further instructions*] Did you tell him I come in a taxi?

MRS PEARCE. Nonsense, girl! what do you think a gentleman like Mr Higgins cares what you came in?

THE FLOWER GIRL. Oh, we are proud! He aint above giving lessons, not him: I heard him say so. Well, I aint come here to ask for any compliment; and if my money's not good enough I can go elsewhere.

HIGGINS. Good enough for what?

THE FLOWER GIRL. Good enough for yə-oo. Now you know, dont you? I'm come to have lessons, I am. And to pay for em tə-oo: make no mistake.

HIGGINS [*stupent*] Well!!! [*Recovering his breath with a gasp*] What do you expect me to say to you?

THE FLOWER GIRL. Well, if you was a gentleman, you might ask me to sit down, I think. Dont I tell you I'm bringing you business?

HIGGINS. Pickering: shall we ask this baggage to sit down, or shall we throw her out of the window?

THE FLOWER GIRL [*running away in terror to the piano, where she turns at bay*] Ah-ah-oh-ow-ow-ow-oo! [*Wounded and whimpering*] I wont be called a baggage when Ive offered to pay like any lady.

Motionless, the two men stare at her from the other side of the room, amazed.

PICKERING [*gently*] But what is it you want?

THE FLOWER GIRL. I want to be a lady in a flower shop stead of sellin at the corner of Tottenham Court Road. But they wont take me unless I can talk more genteel. He said he could teach me. Well, here I am ready to pay him--not asking any favor—and he treats me zif I was dirt.

MRS PEARCE. How can you be such a foolish ignorant girl as to think you could afford to pay Mr Higgins?

THE FLOWER GIRL. Why shouldnt I? I know what lessons cost as well as you do; and I'm ready to pay.

HIGGINS. How much?

THE FLOWER GIRL [*coming back to him, triumphant*] Now youre talking! I thought youd come off it when you saw a chance of getting back a bit of what you chucked at me last night. [*Confidentially*] Youd had a drop in, hadnt you?

HIGGINS [*peremptorily*] Sit down.

THE FLOWER GIRL. Oh, if youre going to make a compliment of it—

HIGGINS [*thundering at her*] Sit down.

MRS PEARCE [*severely*] Sit down, girl. Do as youre told.

THE FLOWER GIRL. Ah-ah-ah-ow-ow-oo! [*She stands, half rebellious, half bewildered*].

PICKERING [*very courteous*] Wont you sit down? [*He places the stray chair near the hearthrug between himself and Higgins*].

THE FLOWER GIRL [*coyly*] Dont mind if I do. [*She sits down. Pickering returns to the hearthrug*].

HIGGINS. Whats your name?

THE FLOWER GIRL. Liza Doolittle.

HIGGINS [*declaiming gravely*]
  Eliza, Elizabeth, Betsy and Bess,
  They went to the woods to get a bird's nes':

PICKERING. They found a nest with four eggs in it:

HIGGINS. They took one apiece, and left three in it.

They laugh heartily at their own fun.

LIZA. Oh, dont be silly.

MRS PEARCE [*placing herself behind Eliza's chair*] You mustnt speak to the gentleman like that.

LIZA. Well, why wont he speak sensible to me?

HIGGINS. Come back to business. How much do you propose to pay me for the lessons?

PYGMALION

LIZA. Oh, I know whats right. A lady friend of mine gets French lessons for eighteenpence an hour from a real French gentleman. Well, you wouldnt have the face to ask me the same for teaching me my own language as you would for French; so I wont give more than a shilling. Take it or leave it.

HIGGINS [*walking up and down the room, rattling his keys and his cash in his pockets*] You know, Pickering, if you consider a shilling, not as a simple shilling, but as a percentage of this girl's income, it works out as fully equivalent to sixty or seventy guineas from a millionaire.

PICKERING. How so?

HIGGINS. Figure it out. A millionaire has about £150 a day. She earns about half-a-crown.

LIZA [*haughtily*] Who told you I only—

HIGGINS [*continuing*] She offers me two-fifths of her day's income for a lesson. Two-fifths of a millionaire's income for a day would be somewhere about £60. It's handsome. By George, it's enormous! it's the biggest offer I ever had.

LIZA [*rising, terrified*] Sixty pounds! What are you talking about? I never offered you sixty pounds. Where would I get—

HIGGINS. Hold your tongue.

LIZA [*weeping*] But I aint got sixty pounds. Oh—

MRS PEARCE. Dont cry, you silly girl. Sit down. Nobody is going to touch your money.

HIGGINS. Somebody is going to touch you, with a broomstick, if you dont stop snivelling. Sit down.

LIZA [*obeying slowly*] Ah-ah-ah-ow-oo-o! One would think you was my father.

HIGGINS. If I decide to teach you, I'll be worse than two fathers to you. Here [*he offers her his silk handkerchief*]!

LIZA. Whats this for?

HIGGINS. To wipe your eyes. To wipe any part of your face that feels moist. Remember: thats your handkerchief; and thats your sleeve. Dont mistake the one for the other if you wish to become a lady in a shop.

Liza, utterly bewildered, stares helplessly at him.

MRS PEARCE. It's no use talking to her like that, Mr Higgins: she doesnt understand you. Besides, youre quite wrong: she doesnt do it that way at all [*she takes the handkerchief*].

LIZA [*snatching it*] Here! You give me that handkerchief. He gev it to me, not to you.

PICKERING [*laughing*] He did. I think it must be regarded as her property, Mrs Pearce.

MRS PEARCE [*resigning herself*] Serve you right, Mr Higgins.

PICKERING. Higgins: I'm interested. What about the ambassador's garden party? I'll say youre the greatest teacher alive if you make that good. I'll bet you all the expenses of the experiment you cant do it. And I'll pay for the lessons.

LIZA. Oh, you are real good. Thank you, Captain.

HIGGINS [*tempted, looking at her*] It's almost irresistible. She's so deliciously low—so horribly dirty—

LIZA [*protesting extremely*] Ah-ah-ah-ah-ow-ow-oo-oo!!! I aint dirty: I washed my face and hands afore I come, I did.

PICKERING. Youre certainly not going to turn her head with flattery, Higgins.

MRS PEARCE [*uneasy*] Oh, dont say that, sir: theres more ways than one of turning a girl's head; and nobody can do it better than Mr Higgins, though he may not always mean it. I do hope, sir, you wont encourage him to do anything foolish.

HIGGINS [*becoming excited as the idea grows on him*] What is life but a series of inspired follies? The difficulty is to find them to do. Never lose a chance: it doesnt come every day. I shall make a duchess of this draggletailed guttersnipe.

LIZA [*strongly deprecating this view of her*] Ah-ah-ah-ow-ow-oo!

HIGGINS [*carried away*] Yes: in six months—in three if she has a good ear and a quick tongue—I'll take her anywhere and pass her off as anything. We'll start today: now! this moment! Take

26

her away and clean her, Mrs Pearce. Monkey Brand, if it wont come off any other way. Is there a good fire in the kitchen?

MRS PEARCE [*protesting*] Yes; but—

HIGGINS [*storming on*] Take all her clothes off and burn them. Ring up Whiteley or somebody for new ones. Wrap her up in brown paper til they come.

LIZA. Youre no gentleman, youre not, to talk of such things. I'm a good girl, I am; and I know what the like of you are, I do.

HIGGINS. We want none of your Lisson Grove prudery here, young woman. Youve got to learn to behave like a duchess. Take her away, Mrs Pearce. If she gives you any trouble, wallop her.

LIZA [*springing up and running between Pickering and Mrs Pearce for protection*] No! I'll call the police, I will.

MRS PEARCE. But Ive no place to put her.

HIGGINS. Put her in the dustbin.

LIZA. Ah-ah-ah-ow-ow-oo!

PICKERING. Oh come, Higgins! be reasonable.

MRS PEARCE [*resolutely*] You m u s t be reasonable, Mr Higgins: really you must. You cant walk over everybody like this.

Higgins, thus scolded, subsides. The hurricane is succeeded by a zephyr of amiable surprise.

HIGGINS [*with professional exquisiteness of modulation*] I walk over everybody! My dear Mrs Pearce, my dear Pickering, I never had the slightest intention of walking over anyone. All I propose is that we should be kind to this poor girl. We must help her to prepare and fit herself for her new station in life. If I did not express myself clearly it was because I did not wish to hurt her delicacy, or yours.

Liza, reassured, steals back to her chair.

MRS PEARCE [*to Pickering*] Well, did you ever hear anything like that, sir?

PICKERING [*laughing heartily*] Never, Mrs Pearce: never.

HIGGINS [*patiently*] Whats the matter?

MRS PEARCE. Well, the matter is, sir, that you cant take a girl up like that as if you were picking up a pebble on the beach.

HIGGINS. Why not?

MRS PEARCE. Why not! But you dont know anything about her. What about her parents? She may be married.

LIZA. Garn!

HIGGINS. There! As the girl very properly says, Garn! Married indeed! Dont you know that a woman of that class looks a worn out drudge of fifty a year after she's married?

LIZA. Whood marry me?

HIGGINS [suddenly resorting to the most thrillingly beautiful low tones in his best elocutionary style] By George, Eliza, the streets will be strewn with the bodies of men shooting themselves for your sake before Ive done with you.

MRS PEARCE. Nonsense, sir. You mustnt talk like that to her.

LIZA [rising and squaring herself determinedly] I'm going away. He's off his chump, he is. I dont want no balmies teaching me.

HIGGINS [wounded in his tenderest point by her insensibility to his elocution] Oh, indeed! I'm mad, am I? Very well, Mrs Pearce: you neednt order the new clothes for her. Throw her out.

LIZA [whimpering] Nah-ow. You got no right to touch me.

MRS PEARCE. You see now what comes of being saucy. [Indicating the door] This way, please.

LIZA [almost in tears] I didnt want no clothes. I wouldnt have taken them [she throws away the handkerchief]. I can buy my own clothes.

HIGGINS [deftly retrieving the handkerchief and intercepting her on her reluctant way to the door] Youre an ungrateful wicked girl. This is my return for offering to take you out of the gutter and dress you beautifully and make a lady of you.

MRS PEARCE. Stop, Mr Higgins. I wont allow it. It's you that are wicked. Go home to your parents, girl; and tell them to take better care of you.

LIZA. I aint got no parents. They told me I was big enough to earn my own living and turned me out.

MRS PEARCE. Wheres your mother?

LIZA. I aint got no mother. Her that turned me out was my sixth stepmother. But I done without them. And I'm a good girl, I am.

HIGGINS. Very well, then, what on earth is all this fuss about? The girl doesnt belong to anybody—is no use to anybody but me. [*He goes to Mrs Pearce and begins coaxing*]. You can adopt her, Mrs Pearce: I'm sure a daughter would be a great amusement to you. Now dont make any more fuss. Take her downstairs; and—

MRS PEARCE. But whats to become of her? Is she to be paid anything? Do be sensible, sir.

HIGGINS. Oh, pay her whatever is necessary: put it down in the housekeeping book. [*Impatiently*] What on earth will she want with money? She'll have her food and her clothes. She'll only drink if you give her money.

LIZA [*turning on him*] Oh you a r e a brute. It's a lie: nobody ever saw the sign of liquor on me. [*To Pickering*] Oh, sir: youre a gentleman: dont let him speak to me like that.

PICKERING [*in good-humoured remonstrance*] Does it occur to you, Higgins, that the girl has some feelings?

HIGGINS [*looking critically at her*] Oh no, I dont think so. Not any feelings that we need bother about. [*Cheerily*] Have you, Eliza?

LIZA. I got my feelings same as anyone else.

HIGGINS [*to Pickering, reflectively*] You see the difficulty?

PICKERING. Eh? What difficulty?

HIGGINS. To get her to talk grammar. The mere pronunciation is easy enough.

LIZA. I dont want to talk grammar. I want to talk like a lady in a flower-shop.

MRS PEARCE. Will you please keep to the point, Mr Higgins. I want to know on what terms the girl is to be here. Is she to have any wages? And what is to become of her when youve finished your teaching? You must look ahead a little.

HIGGINS [*impatiently*] Whats to become of her if I leave her in the gutter? Tell me that, Mrs Pearce.

MRS PEARCE. Thats her own business, not yours, Mr Higgins.

HIGGINS. Well, when Ive done with her, we can throw her back into the gutter; and then it will be her own business again; so thats all right.

LIZA. Oh, youve no feeling heart in you: you dont care for nothing but yourself. [*She rises and takes the floor resolutely*]. Here! Ive had enough of this. I'm going [*making for the door*]. You ought to be ashamed of yourself, you ought.

HIGGINS [*snatching a chocolate cream from the piano, his eyes suddenly beginning to twinkle with mischief*] Have some chocolates, Eliza.

LIZA [*halting, tempted*] How do I know what might be in them? Ive heard of girls being drugged by the like of you.

Higgins whips out his penknife; cuts a chocolate in two; puts one half into his mouth and bolts it; and offers her the other half.

HIGGINS. Pledge of good faith, Eliza. I eat one half: you eat the other. [*Liza opens her mouth to retort: he pops the half chocolate into it*]. You shall have boxes of them, barrels of them, every day. You shall live on them. Eh?

LIZA [*who has disposed of the chocolate after being nearly choked by it*] I wouldnt have ate it, only I'm too ladylike to take it out of my mouth.

HIGGINS. Listen, Eliza. I think you said you came in a taxi.

LIZA. Well, what if I did? Ive as good a right to take a taxi as anyone else.

HIGGINS. You have, Eliza; and in future you shall have as many taxis as you want. You shall go up and down and round the town in a taxi every day. Think of that, Eliza.

MRS PEARCE. Mr Higgins: youre tempting the girl. It's not right. She should think of the future.

HIGGINS. At her age! Nonsense! Time enough to think of the

PYGMALION

future when you havnt any future to think of. No, Eliza: do as this lady does: think of other people's futures; but never think of your own. Think of chocolates, and taxis, and gold, and diamonds.

LIZA. No: I dont want no gold and no diamonds. I'm a good girl, I am. [*She sits down again, with an attempt at dignity*].

HIGGINS. You shall remain so, Eliza, under the care of Mrs Pearce. And you shall marry an officer in the Guards, with a beautiful moustache: the son of a marquis, who will disinherit him for marrying you, but will relent when he sees your beauty and goodness—

PICKERING. Excuse me, Higgins; but I really must interfere. Mrs Pearce is quite right. If this girl is to put herself in your hands for six months for an experiment in teaching, she must understand thoroughly what she's doing.

HIGGINS. How can she? She's incapable of understanding anything. Besides, do any of us understand what we are doing? If we did, would we ever do it?

PICKERING. Very clever, Higgins; but not to the present point. [*To Eliza*] Miss Doolittle—

LIZA [*overwhelmed*] Ah-ah-ow-oo!

HIGGINS. There! Thats all youll get out of Eliza. Ah-ah-ow-oo! No use explaining. As a military man you ought to know that. Give her her orders: thats enough for her. Eliza: you are to live here for the next six months, learning how to speak beautifully, like a lady in a florist's shop. If youre good and do whatever youre told, you shall sleep in a proper bedroom, and have lots to eat, and money to buy chocolates and take rides in taxis. If youre naughty and idle you will sleep in the back kitchen among the black beetles, and be walloped by Mrs Pearce with a broomstick. At the end of six months you shall go to Buckingham Palace in a carriage, beautifully dressed. If the King finds out youre not a lady, you will be taken by the police to the Tower of London. where your head will be cut off as a warning to other presumptuous flower girls. If you are not found out, you shall have a present of seven-and-sixpence to start life with as a lady in a shop. If you refuse this offer you will be a most ungrateful wicked girl; and the angels will weep for you. [*To Pickering*] Now are you satisfied, Pickering? [*To Mrs Pearce*] Can I put it more plainly and fairly, Mrs Pearce?

MRS PEARCE [*patiently*] I think youd better let me speak to the girl properly in private. I dont know that I can take charge of her or consent to the arrangement at all. Of course I know you dont mean her any harm; but when you get what you call interested in people's accents, you never think or care what may happen to them or you. Come with me, Eliza.

HIGGINS. Thats all right. Thank you, Mrs Pearce. Bundle her off to the bath-room.

LIZA [*rising reluctantly and suspiciously*] Youre a great bully, you are. I wont stay here if I dont like. I wont let nobody wallop me. I never asked to go to Bucknam Palace, I didnt. I was never in trouble with the police, not me. I'm a good girl—

MRS PEARCE. Dont answer back, girl. You dont understand the gentleman. Come with me. [*She leads the way to the door, and holds it open for Eliza*].

LIZA [*as she goes out*] Well, what I say is right. I wont go near the King, not if I'm going to have my head cut off. If I'd known what I was letting myself in for, I wouldnt have come here. I always been a good girl; and I never offered to say a word to him; and I dont owe him nothing; and I dont care; and I wont be put upon; and I have my feelings the same as anyone else—

Mrs Pearce shuts the door; and Eliza's plaints are no longer audible.

     *   *   *   *   *   *

Eliza is taken upstairs to the third floor greatly to her surprise; for she expected to be taken down to the scullery. There Mrs Pearce opens a door and takes her into a spare bedroom.

MRS PEARCE. I will have to put you here. This will be your bed-room.

LIZA. O-h, I couldnt sleep here, missus. It's too good for the likes of me. I should be afraid to touch anything. I aint a duchess yet, you know.

MRS PEARCE. You have got to make yourself as clean as the room: then you wont be afraid of it. And you must call me Mrs Pearce, not missus. [*She throws open the door of the dressingroom, now modernized as a bathroom*].

LIZA. Gawd! whats this? Is this where you wash clothes? Funny sort of copper I call it.

MRS PEARCE. It is not a copper. This is where we wash ourselves, Eliza, and where I am going to wash you.

LIZA. You expect me to get into that and wet myself all over! Not me. I should catch my death. I knew a woman did it every Saturday night; and she died of it.

MRS PEARCE. Mr Higgins has the gentlemen's bathroom downstairs; and he has a bath every morning, in cold water.

LIZA. Ugh! He's made of iron, that man.

MRS PEARCE. If you are to sit with him and the Colonel and be taught you will have to do the same. They wont like the smell of you if you dont. But you can have the water as hot as you like. There are two taps: hot and cold.

LIZA [*weeping*] I couldnt. I dursnt. Its not natural: it would kill me. Ive never had a bath in my life: not what youd call a proper one.

MRS PEARCE. Well, dont you want to be clean and sweet and decent, like a lady? You know you cant be a nice girl inside if youre a dirty slut outside.

LIZA. Boohoo!!!!

MRS PEARCE. Now stop crying and go back into your room and take off all your clothes. Then wrap yourself in this [*Taking down a gown from its peg and handing it to her*] and come back to me. I will get the bath ready.

LIZA [*all tears*] I cant. I wont. I'm not used to it. Ive never took off all my clothes before. It's not right: it's not decent.

33

MRS PEARCE. Nonsense, child. Dont you take off all your clothes every night when you go to bed?

LIZA [amazed] No. Why should I? I should catch my death. Of course I take off my skirt.

MRS PEARCE. Do you mean that you sleep in the underclothes you wear in the daytime?

LIZA. What else have I to sleep in?

MRS PEARCE. You will never do that again as long as you live here. I will get you a proper nightdress.

LIZA. Do you mean change into cold things and lie awake shivering half the night? You want to kill me, you do.

MRS PEARCE. I want to change you from a frowzy slut to a clean respectable girl fit to sit with the gentlemen in the study. Are you going to trust me and do what I tell you or be thrown out and sent back to your flower basket?

LIZA. But you dont know what the cold is to me. You dont know how I dread it.

MRS PEARCE. Your bed wont be cold here: I will put a hot water bottle in it. [Pushing her into the bedroom] Off with you and undress.

LIZA. Oh, if only I'd a known what a dreadful thing it is to be clean I'd never have come. I didnt know when I was well off. I— [Mrs Pearce pushes her through the door, but leaves it partly open lest her prisoner should take to flight].

Mrs Pearce puts on a pair of white rubber sleeves, and fills the bath, mixing hot and cold, and testing the result with the bath thermometer. She perfumes it with a handful of bath salts and adds a palmful of mustard. She then takes a formidable looking long handled scrubbing brush and soaps it profusely with a ball of scented soap.

Eliza comes back with nothing on but the bath gown huddled tightly round her, a piteous spectacle of abject terror.

MRS PEARCE. Now come along. Take that thing off.

LIZA. Oh I couldnt, Mrs Pearce: I reely couldnt. I never done such a thing.

MRS PEARCE. Nonsense. Here: step in and tell me whether its hot enough for you.

LIZA. Ah-oo! Ah-oo! It's too hot.

MRS PEARCE [*deftly snatching the gown away and throwing Eliza down on her back*] It wont hurt you. [*She sets to work with the scrubbing brush*].

Eliza's screams are heartrending.

* * * * * *

Meanwhile the Colonel has been having it out with Higgins about Eliza. Pickering has come from the hearth to the chair and seated himself astride of it with his arms on the back to cross-examine him.

PICKERING. Excuse the straight question, Higgins. Are you a man of good character where women are concerned?

HIGGINS [*moodily*] Have you ever met a man of good character where women are concerned?

PICKERING. Yes: very frequently.

HIGGINS [*dogmatically, lifting himself on his hands to the level of the piano, and sitting on it with a bounce*] Well, I havnt. I find that the moment I let a woman make friends with me, she becomes jealous, exacting, suspicious, and a damned nuisance. I find that the moment I let myself make friends with a woman, I become selfish and tyrannical. Women upset everything. When you let them into your life, you find that the woman is driving at one thing and youre driving at another.

PICKERING. At what, for example?

HIGGINS [*coming off the piano restlessly*] Oh, Lord knows! I suppose the woman wants to live her own life; and the man wants to live his; and each tries to drag the other on to the wrong track. One wants to go north and the other south; and the result is that both have to go east, though they both hate the east wind. [*He sits down on the bench at the keyboard*]. So here I am, a confirmed old bachelor, and likely to remain so.

PICKERING [*rising and standing over him gravely*] Come, Hig-

PYGMALION

gins! You know what I mean. If I'm to be in this business I shall feel responsible for that girl. I hope it's understood that no advantage is to be taken of her position.

HIGGINS. What! That thing! Sacred, I assure you. [*Rising to explain*] You see, she'll be a pupil; and teaching would be impossible unless pupils were sacred. Ive taught scores of American millionairesses how to speak English: the best looking women in the world. I'm seasoned. They might as well be blocks of wood. *I* might as well be a block of wood. It's—

Mrs Pearce opens the door. She has Eliza's hat in her hand. Pickering retires to the easy-chair at the hearth and sits down.

HIGGINS [*eagerly*] Well, Mrs Pearce: is it all right?

MRS PEARCE [*at the door*] I just wish to trouble you with a word, if I may, Mr Higgins.

HIGGINS. Yes, certainly. Come in. [*She comes forward*]. Dont burn that, Mrs Pearce. I'll keep it as a curiosity. [*He takes the hat*].

MRS PEARCE. Handle it carefully, sir, p l e a s e. I had to promise her not to burn it; but I had better put it in the oven for a while.

HIGGINS [*putting it down hastily on the piano*] Oh! thank you. Well, what have you to say to me?

PICKERING. Am I in the way?

MRS PEARCE. Not at all, sir. Mr. Higgins: will you please be very particular what you say before the girl?

HIGGINS [*sternly*] Of course. I'm always particular about what I say. Why do you say this to me?

MRS PEARCE [*unmoved*] No, sir: youre not at all particular when youve mislaid anything or when you get a little impatient. Now it doesnt matter before me: I'm used to it. But you really must not swear before the girl.

HIGGINS [*indignantly*] *I* swear! [*Most emphatically*] I never swear. I detest the habit. What the devil do you mean?

MRS PEARCE [*stolidly*] Thats what I mean, sir. You swear a great deal too much. I dont mind your damning and blasting, and w h a t the devil and w h e r e the devil and w h o the devil—

36

HIGGINS. Mrs Pearce: this language from your lips! Really!

MRS PEARCE [*not to be put off*]—but there is a certain word I must ask you not to use. The girl used it herself when she began to enjoy the bath. It begins with the same letter as bath. She knows no better: she learnt it at her mother's knee. But she must not hear it from your lips.

HIGGINS [*loftily*] I cannot charge myself with having ever uttered it, Mrs Pearce. [*She looks at him steadfastly. He adds, hiding an uneasy conscience with a judicial air*] Except perhaps in a moment of extreme and justifiable excitement.

MRS PEARCE. Only this morning, sir, you applied it to your boots, to the butter, and to the brown bread.

HIGGINS. Oh, that! Mere alliteration, Mrs Pearce, natural to a poet.

MRS PEARCE. Well, sir, whatever you choose to call it, I beg you not to let the girl hear you repeat it.

HIGGINS. Oh, very well, very well. Is that all?

MRS PEARCE. No, sir. We shall have to be very particular with this girl as to personal cleanliness.

HIGGINS. Certainly. Quite right. Most important.

MRS PEARCE. I mean not to be slovenly about her dress or untidy in leaving things about.

HIGGINS [*going to her solemnly*] Just so. I intended to call your attention to that. [*He passes on to Pickering, who is enjoying the conversation immensely*]. It is these little things that matter, Pickering. Take care of the pence and the pounds will take care of themselves is as true of personal habits as of money. [*He comes to anchor on the hearthrug, with the air of a man in an unassailable position*].

MRS PEARCE. Yes, sir. Then might I ask you not to come down to breakfast in your dressing-gown, or at any rate not to use it as a napkin to the extent you do, sir. And if you would be so good as not to eat everything off the same plate, and to remember not to put the porridge saucepan out of your hand on the clean table-

PYGMALION

cloth, it would be a better example to the girl. You know you nearly choked yourself with a fishbone in the jam only last week.

HIGGINS [*routed from the hearthrug and drifting back to the piano*] I may do these things sometimes in absence of mind; but surely I dont do them habitually. [*Angrily*] By the way: my dressing-gown smells most damnably of benzine.

MRS PEARCE. No doubt it does, Mr Higgins. But if you will wipe your fingers—

HIGGINS [*yelling*] Oh very well, very well: I'll wipe them in my hair in future.

MRS PEARCE. I hope youre not offended, Mr Higgins.

HIGGINS [*shocked at finding himself thought capable of an unamiable sentiment*] Not at all, not at all. Youre quite right, Mrs Pearce: I shall be particularly careful before the girl. Is that all?

MRS PEARCE. No, sir. Might she use some of those Japanese dresses you brought from abroad? I really cant put her back into her old things.

HIGGINS. Certainly. Anything you like. Is t h a t all?

MRS PEARCE. Thank you, sir. Thats all. [*She goes out*].

HIGGINS. You know, Pickering, that woman has the most extraordinary ideas about me. Here I am, a shy, diffident sort of man. Ive never been able to feel really grown-up and tremendous, like other chaps. And yet she's firmly persuaded that I'm an arbitrary overbearing bossing kind of person. I cant account for it.

Mrs Pearce returns.

MRS PEARCE. If you please, sir, the trouble's beginning already. Theres a dustman downstairs, Alfred Doolittle, wants to see you. He says you have his daughter here.

PICKERING [*rising*] Phew! I say!

HIGGINS [*promptly*] Send the blackguard up.

MRS PEARCE. Oh, very well, sir. [*She goes out*].

PICKERING. He may not be a blackguard, Higgins.

HIGGINS. Nonsense. Of course he's a blackguard.

38

PICKERING. Whether he is or not, I'm afraid we shall have some trouble with him.

HIGGINS [*confidently*] Oh no: I think not. If theres any trouble he shall have it with me, not I with him. And we are sure to get something interesting out of him.

PICKERING. About the girl?

HIGGINS. No. I mean his dialect.

PICKERING. Oh!

MRS PEARCE [*at the door*] Doolittle, sir. [*She admits Doolittle and retires*].

Alfred Doolittle is an elderly but vigorous dustman, clad in the costume of his profession, including a hat with a back brim covering his neck and shoulders. He has well marked and rather interesting features, and seems equally free from fear and conscience. He has a remarkably expressive voice, the result of a habit of giving vent to his feelings without reserve. His present pose is that of wounded honor and stern resolution.

DOOLITTLE [*at the door, uncertain which of the two gentlemen is his man*] Professor Iggins?

HIGGINS. Here. Good morning. Sit down.

DOOLITTLE. Morning, Governor. [*He sits down magisterially*] I come about a very serious matter, Governor.

HIGGINS [*to Pickering*] Brought up in Hounslow. Mother Welsh, I should think. [*Doolittle opens his mouth, amazed. Higgins continues*] What do you want, Doolittle?

DOOLITTLE [*menacingly*] I want my daughter: thats what I want. See?

HIGGINS. Of course you do. Youre her father, arnt you? You dont suppose anyone else wants her, do you? I'm glad to see you have some spark of family feeling left. She's upstairs. Take her away at once.

DOOLITTLE [*rising, fearfully taken aback*] What.

HIGGINS. Take her away. Do you suppose I'm going to keep your daughter for you?

DOOLITTLE [*remonstrating*] Now, now, look here, Governor. Is this reasonable? Is it fairity to take advantage of a man like this? The girl belongs to me. You got her. Where do I come in? [*He sits down again*].

HIGGINS. Your daughter had the audacity to come to my house and ask me to teach her how to speak properly so that she could get a place in a flower-shop. This gentleman and my housekeeper have been here all the time. [*Bullying him*] How dare you come here and attempt to blackmail me? You sent her here on purpose.

DOOLITTLE [*protesting*] No, Governor.

HIGGINS. You must have. How else could you possibly know that she is here?

DOOLITTLE. Dont take a man up like that, Governor.

HIGGINS. The police shall take you up. This is a plant—a plot to extort money by threats. I shall telephone for the police [*he goes resolutely to the telephone and opens the directory*].

DOOLITTLE. Have I asked you for a brass farthing? I leave it to the gentleman here: have I said a word about money?

HIGGINS [*throwing the book aside and marching down on Doolittle with a poser*] What else did you come for?

DOOLITTLE [*sweetly*] Well, what would a man come for? Be human, Governor.

HIGGINS [*disarmed*] Alfred: did you put her up to it?

DOOLITTLE. So help me, Governor, I never did. I take my Bible oath I aint seen the girl these two months past.

HIGGINS. Then how did you know she was here?

DOOLITTLE ["*most musical, most melancholy*"] I'll tell you, Governor, if youll only let me get a word in. I'm willing to tell you. I'm wanting to tell you. I'm waiting to tell you.

HIGGINS. Pickering: this chap has a certain natural gift of rhetoric. Observe the rhythm of his native woodnotes wild. "I'm willing to tell you: I'm wanting to tell you: I'm waiting to tell you." Sentimental rhetoric! thats the Welsh strain in him. It also accounts for his mendacity and dishonesty.

PYGMALION

PICKERING. Oh, p l e a s e, Higgins: I'm west country myself. [*To Doolittle*] How did you know the girl was here if you didnt send her?

DOOLITTLE. It was like this, Governor. The girl took a boy in the taxi to give him a jaunt. Son of her landlady, he is. He hung about on the chance of her giving him another ride home. Well, she sent him back for her luggage when she heard you was willing for her to stop here. I met the boy at the corner of Long Acre and Endell Street.

HIGGINS. Public house. Yes?

DOOLITTLE. The poor man's club, Governor: why shouldnt I?

PICKERING. Do let him tell his story, Higgins.

DOOLITTLE. He told me what was up. And I ask you, what was my feelings and my duty as a father? I says to the boy, "You bring me the luggage," I says—

PICKERING. Why didnt you go for it yourself?

DOOLITTLE. Landlady wouldnt have trusted me with it, Governor. She's that kind of woman: y o u know. I had to give the boy a penny afore h e trusted me with it, the little swine. I brought it to her just to oblige you like, and make myself agreeable. Thats all.

HIGGINS. How much luggage?

DOOLITTLE. Musical instrument, Governor. A few pictures, a trifle of jewelry, and a bird-cage. She said she didnt want no clothes. What was I to think from that, Governor? I ask you as a parent what was I to think?

HIGGINS. So you came to rescue her from worse than death, eh?

DOOLITTLE [*appreciatively: relieved at being so well understood*] Just so, Governor. Thats right.

PICKERING. But why did you bring her luggage if you intended to take her away?

DOOLITTLE. Have I said a word about taking her away? Have I now?

PYGMALION

HIGGINS [*determinedly*] Youre going to take her away, double quick. [*He crosses to the hearth and rings the bell*].

DOOLITTLE [*rising*] No, Governor. Dont say that. I'm not the man to stand in my girl's light. Heres a career opening for her, as you might say; and—

Mrs Pearce opens the door and awaits orders.

HIGGINS. Mrs Pearce: this is Eliza's father. He has come to take her away. Give her to him. [*He goes back to the piano, with an air of washing his hands of the whole affair*].

DOOLITTLE. No. This is a misunderstanding. Listen here—

MRS PEARCE. He cant take her away, Mr Higgins: how can he? You told me to burn her clothes.

DOOLITTLE. Thats right. I cant carry the girl through the streets like a blooming monkey, can I? I put it to you.

HIGGINS. You have put it to me that you want your daughter. Take your daughter. If she has no clothes go out and buy her some.

DOOLITTLE [*desperate*] Wheres the clothes she came in? Did I burn them or did your missus here?

MRS PEARCE. I am the housekeeper, if you please. I have sent for some clothes for your girl. When they come you can take her away. You can wait in the kitchen. This way, please.

Doolittle, much troubled, accompanies her to the door; then hesitates; finally turns confidentially to Higgins.

DOOLITTLE. Listen here, Governor. You and me is men of the world, aint we?

HIGGINS. Oh! Men of the world, are we? Youd better go, Mrs Pearce.

MRS PEARCE. I think so, indeed, sir. [*She goes, with dignity*].

PICKERING. The floor is yours, Mr Doolittle.

DOOLITTLE [*to Pickering*] I thank you, Governor. [*To Higgins, who takes refuge on the piano bench, a little overwhelmed by the proximity of his visitor, for Doolittle has a professional flavor of dust about him*]. Well, the truth is, Ive taken a sort of fancy to you,

Governor; and if you want the girl, I'm not so set on having her back home again but what I might be open to an arrangement. Regarded in the light of a young woman, she's a fine handsome girl. As a daughter she's not worth her keep; and so I tell you straight. All I ask is my rights as a father; and youre the last man alive to expect me to let her go for nothing; for I can see youre one of the straight sort, Governor. Well, whats a five-pound note to you? and whats Eliza to me? [*He turns to his chair and sits down judicially*].

PICKERING. I think you ought to know, Doolittle, that Mr Higgins's intentions are entirely honorable.

DOOLITTLE. Course they are, Governor. If I thought they wasnt, I'd ask fifty.

HIGGINS [*revolted*] Do you mean to say that you would sell your daughter for £50?

DOOLITTLE. Not in a general way I wouldnt; but to oblige a gentleman like you I'd do a good deal, I do assure you.

PICKERING. Have you no morals, man?

DOOLITTLE [*unabashed*] Cant afford them, Governor. Neither could you if you was as poor as me. Not that I mean any harm, you know. But if Liza is going to have a bit out of this, why not me too?

HIGGINS [*troubled*] I dont know what to do, Pickering. There can be no question that as a matter of morals it's a positive crime to give this chap a farthing. And yet I feel a sort of rough justice in his claim.

DOOLITTLE. Thats it, Governor. Thats all I say. A father's heart, as it were.

PICKERING. Well, I know the feeling; but really it seems hardly right—

DOOLITTLE. Dont say that, Governor. Dont look at it that way. What am I, Governors both? I ask you, what am I? I'm one of the undeserving poor: thats what I am. Think of what that means to a man. It means that he's up agen middle class morality all the time. If theres anything going, and I put in for a bit of it, it's always the same story: "Youre undeserving; so you cant have it." But my needs is as great as the most deserving widow's that ever got money out of six different charities in one week for the death of the same husband. I dont need less than a deserving man: I need more. I dont eat less hearty than him; and I drink a lot more. I want a bit of amusement, cause I'm a thinking man. I want cheerfulness and a song and a band when I feel low. Well, they charge me just the same for everything as they charge the deserving. What is middle class morality? Just an excuse for never giving me anything. Therefore, I ask you, as two gentlemen, not to play that game on me. I'm playing straight with you. I aint pretending to be deserving. I'm undeserving; and I mean to go on being undeserving. I like it; and thats the truth. Will you take advantage of a man's nature to do him out of the price of his own daughter what he's brought up and fed and clothed by the sweat of his brow until she's growed big enough to be interesting to you two gentlemen? Is five pounds unreasonable? I put it to you; and I leave it to you.

HIGGINS [*rising, and going over to Pickering*] Pickering: if we were to take this man in hand for three months, he could choose between a seat in the Cabinet and a popular pulpit in Wales.

PICKERING. What do you say to that, Doolittle?

DOOLITTLE. Not me, Governor, thank you kindly. Ive heard all the preachers and all the prime ministers—for I'm a thinking man and game for politics or religion or social reform same as all the other amusements—and I tell you it's a dog's life any way you look at it. Undeserving poverty is my line. Taking one station in society with another, it's—it's—well, it's the only one that has any ginger in it, to my taste.

HIGGINS. I suppose we must give him a fiver.

PICKERING. He'll make a bad use of it, I'm afraid.

DOOLITTLE. Not me, Governor, so help me I wont. Dont you be afraid that I'll save it and spare it and live idle on it. There

PYGMALION

wont be a penny of it left by Monday: I'll have to go to work same as if I'd never had it. It wont pauperize me, you bet. Just one good spree for myself and the missus, giving pleasure to ourselves and employment to others, and satisfaction to you to think it's not been throwed away. You couldnt spend it better.

HIGGINS [*taking out his pocket book and coming between Doolittle and the piano*] This is irresistible. Lets give him ten. [*He offers two notes to the dustman*].

DOOLITTLE. No, Governor. She wouldnt have the heart to spend ten; and perhaps I shouldnt neither. Ten pounds is a lot of money: it makes a man feel prudent like; and then goodbye to happiness. You give me what I ask you, Governor: not a penny more, and not a penny less.

PICKERING. Why dont you marry that missus of yours? I rather draw the line at encouraging that sort of immorality.

DOOLITTLE. Tell her so, Governor: tell her so. *I*'m willing. It's me that suffers by it. Ive no hold on her. I got to be agreeable to her. I got to give her presents. I got to buy her clothes something sinful. I'm a slave to that woman, Governor, just because I'm not her lawful husband. And she knows it too. Catch her marrying me! Take my advice, Governor: marry Eliza while she's young and dont know no better. If you dont youll be sorry for it after. If you do, she'll be sorry for it after; but better her than you, because youre a man, and she's only a woman and dont know how to be happy anyhow.

HIGGINS. Pickering: if we listen to this man another minute, we shall have no convictions left. [*To Doolittle*] Five pounds I think you said.

DOOLITTLE. Thank you kindly, Governor.

HIGGINS. Youre sure you wont take ten?

DOOLITTLE. Not now. Another time, Governor.

HIGGINS [*handing him a five-pound note*] Here you are.

DOOLITTLE. Thank you, Governor. Good morning. [*He hurries to the door, anxious to get away with his booty. When he opens it he*

45

PYGMALION

is confronted with a dainty and exquisitely clean young Japanese lady in a simple blue cotton kimono printed cunningly with small white jasmine blossoms. Mrs Pearce is with her. He gets out of her way deferentially and apologizes]. Beg pardon, miss.

THE JAPANESE LADY. Garn! Dont you know your own daughter?

DOOLITTLE *exclaiming* Bly me! it's Eliza!
HIGGINS *simul-* Whats that? This!
PICKERING *taneously* By Jove!

LIZA. Dont I look silly?

HIGGINS. Silly?

MRS PEARCE [*at the door*] Now, Mr Higgins, please dont say anything to make the girl conceited about herself.

HIGGINS [*conscientiously*] Oh! Quite right, Mrs Pearce. [*To Eliza*] Yes: damned silly.

MRS PEARCE. Please, sir.

HIGGINS [*correcting himself*] I mean extremely silly.

LIZA. I should look all right with my hat on. [*She takes up her hat; puts it on; and walks across the room to the fireplace with a fashionable air*].

HIGGINS. A new fashion, by George! And it ought to look horrible!

DOOLITTLE [*with fatherly pride*] Well, I never thought she'd clean up as good looking as that, Governor. She's a credit to me, aint she?

LIZA. I tell you, it's easy to clean up here. Hot and cold water on tap, just as much as you like, there is. Woolly towels, there is; and a towel horse so hot, it burns your fingers. Soft brushes to scrub yourself, and a wooden bowl of soap smelling like primroses. Now I know why ladies is so clean. Washing's a treat for them. Wish they could see what it is for the like of me!

HIGGINS. I'm glad the bathroom met with your approval.

LIZA. It didnt: not all of it; and I dont care who hears me say it. Mrs Pearce knows.

HIGGINS. What was wrong, Mrs Pearce?

MRS PEARCE [*blandly*] Oh, nothing, sir. It doesnt matter.

LIZA. I had a good mind to break it. I didnt know which way to look. But I hung a towel over it, I did.

HIGGINS. Over what?

MRS PEARCE. Over the looking-glass, sir.

HIGGINS. Doolittle: you have brought your daughter up too strictly.

DOOLITTLE. Me! I never brought her up at all, except to give her a lick of a strap now and again. Dont put it on me, Governor. She aint accustomed to it, you see: thats all. But she'll soon pick up your free-and-easy ways.

LIZA. I'm a good girl, I am; and I wont pick up no free-and-easy ways.

HIGGINS. Eliza: if you say again that youre a good girl, your father shall take you home.

LIZA. Not him. You dont know my father. All he come here for was to touch you for some money to get drunk on.

DOOLITTLE. Well, what else would I want money for? To put into the plate in church, I suppose. [*She puts out her tongue at him. He is so incensed by this that Pickering presently finds it necessary to step between them*]. Dont you give me none of your lip; and dont let me hear you giving this gentleman any of it neither, or youll hear from me about it. See?

HIGGINS. Have you any further advice to give her before you go, Doolittle? Your blessing, for instance.

DOOLITTLE. No, Governor: I aint such a mug as to put up my children to all I know myself. Hard enough to hold them in without that. If you want Eliza's mind improved, Governor, you do it yourself with a strap. So long, gentlemen. [*He turns to go*].

HIGGINS [*impressively*] Stop. Youll come regularly to see your daughter. It's your duty, you know. My brother is a clergyman; and he could help you in your talks with her.

DOOLITTLE [*evasively*] Certainly, I'll come, Governor. Not just this week, because I have a job at a distance. But later on you may depend on me. Afternoon, gentlemen. Afternoon, maam. [*He touches his hat to Mrs Pearce, who disdains the salutation and goes out. He winks at Higgins, thinking him probably a fellow-sufferer from Mrs Pearce's difficult disposition, and follows her*].

LIZA. Dont you believe the old liar. He'd as soon you set a bulldog on him as a clergyman. You wont see him again in a hurry.

HIGGINS. I dont want to, Eliza. Do you?

LIZA. Not me. I dont want never to see him again, I dont. He's a disgrace to me, he is, collecting dust, instead of working at his trade.

PICKERING. What is his trade, Eliza?

LIZA. Talking money out of other people's pockets into his own. His proper trade's a navvy; and he works at it sometimes too—for exercise—and earns good money at it. Aint you going to call me Miss Doolittle any more?

PICKERING. I beg your pardon, Miss Doolittle. It was a slip of the tongue.

LIZA. Oh, I dont mind; only it sounded so genteel. I should just like to take a taxi to the corner of Tottenham Court Road and get out there and tell it to wait for me, just to put the girls in their place a bit. I wouldnt speak to them, you know.

PICKERING. Better wait til we get you something really fashionable.

HIGGINS. Besides, you shouldnt cut your old friends now that you have risen in the world. Thats what we call snobbery.

LIZA. You dont call the like of them my friends now, I should hope. Theyve took it out of me often enough with their ridicule when they had the chance; and now I mean to get a bit of my own back. But if I'm to have fashionable clothes, I'll wait. I should like to have some. Mrs Pearce says youre going to give me some to wear in bed at night different to what I wear in the daytime; but it do seem a waste of money when you could get something to shew. Besides, I never could fancy changing into cold things on a winter night.

MRS PEARCE [coming back] Now, Eliza. The new things have come for you to try on.

LIZA. Ah-ow-oo-ooh! [She rushes out].

MRS PEARCE [following her] Oh, dont rush about like that, girl. [She shuts the door behind her].

HIGGINS. Pickering: we have taken on a stiff job.

PICKERING [with conviction] Higgins: we have.

       *   *   *   *   *   *

There seems to be some curiosity as to what Higgins's lessons to Eliza were like. Well, here is a sample: the first one.

Picture Eliza, in her new clothes, and feeling her inside put out of step by a lunch, dinner, and breakfast of a kind to which it is unaccustomed, seated with Higgins and the Colonel in the study, feeling like a hospital out-patient at a first encounter with the doctors.

Higgins, constitutionally unable to sit still, discomposes her still more by striding restlessly about. But for the reassuring presence and quietude of her friend the Colonel she would run for her life, even back to Drury Lane.

HIGGINS. Say your alphabet.

LIZA. I know my alphabet. Do you think I know nothing? I dont need to be taught like a child.

HIGGINS [thundering] Say your alphabet.

PICKERING. Say it, Miss Doolittle. You will understand presently. Do what he tells you; and let him teach you in his own way.

LIZA. Oh well, if you put it like that—Ahyee, bɔyee, cɔyee, dɔyee—

HIGGINS [with the roar of a wounded lion] Stop. Listen to this, Pickering. This is what we pay for as elementary education. This unfortunate animal has been locked up for nine years in school at our expense to teach her to speak and read the language of

Shakespear and Milton. And the result is Ahyee, Bə-yee, Cə-yee, Də-yee. [*To Eliza*] Say A, B, C, D.

LIZA [*almost in tears*] But I'm sayin it. Ahyee, Bəyee, Cə-yee—

HIGGINS. Stop. Say a cup of tea.

LIZA. A cappətə-ee.

HIGGINS. Put your tongue forward until it squeezes against the top of your lower teeth. Now say cup.

LIZA. C-c-c—I cant. C-Cup.

PICKERING. Good. Splendid, Miss Doolittle.

HIGGINS. By Jupiter, she's done it at the first shot. Pickering: we shall make a duchess of her. [*To Eliza*] Now do you think you could possibly say tea? Not tə-yee, mind: if you ever say bə-yee cə-yee də-yee again you shall be dragged round the room three times by the hair of your head. [*Fortissimo*] T, T, T, T.

LIZA [*weeping*] I cant hear no difference cep that it sounds more genteel-like when you say it.

HIGGINS. Well, if you can hear that difference, what the devil are you crying for? Pickering: give her a chocolate.

PICKERING. No no. Never mind crying a little, Miss Doolittle: you are doing very well; and the lessons wont hurt. I promise you I wont let him drag you round the room by your hair.

HIGGINS. Be off with you to Mrs Pearce and tell her about it. Think about it. Try to do it by yourself: and keep your tongue well forward in your mouth instead of trying to roll it up and swallow it. Another lesson at half-past four this afternoon. Away with you.

Eliza, still sobbing, rushes from the room.

And that is the sort of ordeal poor Eliza has to go through for months before we meet her again on her first appearance in London society of the professional class.

ACT III

It is Mrs Higgins's at-home day. Nobody has yet arrived. Her drawing room, in a flat on Chelsea Embankment, has three windows looking on the river; and the ceiling is not so lofty as it would be in an older house of the same pretension. The windows are open, giving access to a balcony with flowers in pots. If you stand with your face to the windows, you have the fireplace on your left and the door in the right-hand wall close to the corner nearest the windows.

Mrs Higgins was brought up on Morris and Burne Jones; and her room, which is very unlike her son's room in Wimpole Street, is not crowded with furniture and little tables and nicknacks. In the middle of the room there is a big ottoman; and this, with the carpet, the Morris wall-papers, and the Morris chintz window curtains and brocade covers of the ottoman and its cushions, supply all the ornament, and are much too handsome to be hidden by odds and ends of useless things. A few good oil-paintings from the exhibitions in the Grosvenor Gallery thirty years ago (the Burne Jones, not the Whistler side of them) are on the walls. The only landscape is a Cecil Lawson on the scale of a Rubens. There is a portrait of Mrs Higgins as she was when she defied fashion in her youth in one of the beautiful Rossettian costumes which, when caricatured by people who did not understand, led to the absurdities of popular estheticism in the eighteen-seventies.

In the corner diagonally opposite the door Mrs Higgins, now over sixty and long past taking the trouble to dress out of the fashion, sits writing at an elegantly simple writing-table with a bell button within reach of her hand. There is a Chippendale chair further back in the room between her and the window nearest her side. At the other side of the room, further forward, is an Elizabethan chair roughly carved in the taste of Inigo Jones. On the same side a piano in a decorated case. The corner between the fireplace and the window is occupied by a divan cushioned in Morris chintz.

51

PYGMALION

It is between four and five in the afternoon.
The door is opened violently; and Higgins enters with his hat on.

MRS HIGGINS [*dismayed*] Henry! [*Scolding him*] What are you doing here today? It is my at-home day: you promised not to come. [*As he bends to kiss her, she takes his hat off, and presents it to him*].

HIGGINS. Oh bother! [*He throws the hat down on the table*].

MRS HIGGINS. Go home at once.

HIGGINS [*kissing her*] I know, mother. I came on purpose.

MRS HIGGINS. But you mustnt. I'm serious, Henry. You offend all my friends: they stop coming whenever they meet you.

HIGGINS. Nonsense! I know I have no small talk; but people dont mind. [*He sits on the settee*].

MRS HIGGINS. Oh! dont they? Small talk indeed! What about your large talk? Really, dear, you mustnt stay.

HIGGINS. I must. Ive a job for you. A phonetic job.

MRS HIGGINS. No use, dear. I'm sorry; but I cant get round your vowels; and though I like to get pretty postcards in your patent shorthand, I always have to read the copies in ordinary writing you so thoughtfully send me.

HIGGINS. Well, this isnt a phonetic job.

MRS HIGGINS. You said it was.

HIGGINS. Not your part of it. Ive picked up a girl.

MRS HIGGINS. Does that mean that some girl has picked y o u up?

HIGGINS. Not at all. I dont mean a love affair.

MRS HIGGINS. What a pity!

HIGGINS. Why?

MRS HIGGINS. Well, you never fall in love with anyone under forty-five. When will you discover that there are some rather nice-looking young women about?

HIGGINS. Oh, I cant be bothered with young women. My idea of a lovable woman is somebody as like you as possible. I shall never get into the way of seriously liking young women: some

52

habits lie too deep to be changed. [*Rising abruptly and walking about, jingling his money and his keys in his trouser pockets*] Besides, theyre all idiots.

MRS HIGGINS. Do you know what you would do if you really loved me, Henry?

HIGGINS. Oh bother! What? Marry, I suppose.

MRS HIGGINS. No. Stop fidgeting and take your hands out of your pockets. [*With a gesture of despair, he obeys and sits down again*]. Thats a good boy. Now tell me about the girl.

HIGGINS. She's coming to see you.

MRS HIGGINS. I dont remember asking her.

HIGGINS. You didnt. *I* asked her. If youd known her you wouldnt have asked her.

MRS HIGGINS. Indeed! Why?

HIGGINS. Well, it's like this. She's a common flower girl. I picked her off the kerbstone.

MRS HIGGINS. And invited her to my at-home!

HIGGINS [*rising and coming to her to coax her*] Oh, thatll be all right. Ive taught her to speak properly; and she has strict orders as to her behavior. She's to keep to two subjects: the weather and everybody's health—Fine day and How do you do, you know —and not to let herself go on things in general. That will be safe.

MRS HIGGINS. Safe! To talk about our health! about our insides! perhaps about our outsides! How could you be so silly, Henry?

HIGGINS [*impatiently*] Well, she must talk about something. [*He controls himself and sits down again*]. Oh, she'll be all right: dont you fuss. Pickering is in it with me. Ive a sort of bet on that I'll pass her off as a duchess in six months. I started on her some months ago; and she's getting on like a house on fire. I shall win my bet. She has a quick ear; and she's been easier to teach than my middle-class pupils because she's had to learn a complete new language. She talks English almost as you talk French.

MRS HIGGINS. Thats satisfactory, at all events.

HIGGINS. Well, it is and it isnt.

MRS HIGGINS. What does that mean?

HIGGINS. You see, Ive got her pronunciation all right; but you have to consider not only how a girl pronounces, but what she pronounces; and that's where—

They are interrupted by the parlor-maid, announcing guests.

THE PARLOR-MAID. Mrs and Miss Eynsford Hill. [*She withdraws*].

HIGGINS. Oh Lord! [*He rises; snatches his hat from the table; and makes for the door; but before he reaches it his mother introduces him*].

Mrs and Miss Eynsford Hill are the mother and daughter who sheltered from the rain in Covent Garden. The mother is well bred, quiet, and has the habitual anxiety of straitened means. The daughter has acquired a gay air of being very much at home in society: the bravado of genteel poverty.

MRS EYNSFORD HILL [*to Mrs Higgins*] How do you do? [*They shake hands*].

MISS EYNSFORD HILL. How d'you do? [*She shakes*].

MRS HIGGINS [*introducing*] My son Henry.

MRS EYNSFORD HILL. Your celebrated son! I have so longed to meet you, Professor Higgins.

HIGGINS [*glumly, making no movement in her direction*] Delighted. [*He backs against the piano and bows brusquely*].

MISS EYNSFORD HILL [*going to him with confident familiarity*] How do you do?

HIGGINS [*staring at her*] Ive seen you before somewhere. I havnt the ghost of a notion where; but Ive heard your voice. [*Drearily*] It doesnt matter. Youd better sit down.

MRS HIGGINS. I'm sorry to say that my celebrated son has no manners. You mustnt mind him.

MISS EYNSFORD HILL [*gaily*] I dont. [*She sits in the Elizabethan chair*].

PYGMALION

MRS EYNSFORD HILL [*a little bewildered*] Not at all. [*She sits on the ottoman between her daughter and Mrs Higgins, who has turned her chair away from the writing-table*].

HIGGINS. Oh, have I been rude? I didnt mean to be.

He goes to the central window, through which, with his back to the company, he contemplates the river and the flowers in Battersea Park on the opposite bank as if they were a frozen desert.

The parlor-maid returns, ushering in Pickering.

THE PARLOR-MAID. Colonel Pickering. [*She withdraws*].

PICKERING. How do you do, Mrs Higgins?

MRS HIGGINS. So glad youve come. Do you know Mrs Eynsford Hill—Miss Eynsford Hill? [*Exchange of bows. The Colonel brings the Chippendale chair a little forward between Mrs Hill and Mrs Higgins, and sits down*].

PICKERING. Has Henry told you what weve come for?

HIGGINS [*over his shoulder*] We were interrupted: damn it!

MRS HIGGINS. Oh Henry, Henry, really!

MRS EYNSFORD HILL [*half rising*] Are we in the way?

MRS HIGGINS [*rising and making her sit down again*] No, no. You couldnt have come more fortunately: we want you to meet a friend of ours.

HIGGINS [*turning hopefully*] Yes, by George! We want two or three people. Youll do as well as anybody else.

The parlor-maid returns, ushering Freddy.

THE PARLOR-MAID. Mr Eynsford Hill.

HIGGINS [*almost audibly, past endurance*] God of Heaven! another of them.

FREDDY [*shaking hands with Mrs Higgins*] Ahdedo?

MRS HIGGINS. Very good of you to come. [*Introducing*] Colonel Pickering.

FREDDY [*bowing*] Ahdedo?

MRS HIGGINS. I dont think you know my son, Professor Higgins.

FREDDY [*going to Higgins*] Ahdedo?

PYGMALION

HIGGINS [*looking at him much as if he were a pickpocket*] I'll take my oath Ive met you before somewhere. Where was it?

FREDDY. I dont think so.

HIGGINS [*resignedly*] It dont matter, anyhow. Sit down.

He shakes Freddy's hand, and almost slings him on to the ottoman with his face to the windows; then comes round to the other side of it.

HIGGINS. Well, here we are, anyhow! [*He sits down on the ottoman next Mrs Eynsford Hill, on her left*]. And now, what the devil are we going to talk about until Eliza comes?

MRS HIGGINS. Henry: you are the life and soul of the Royal Society's soirees; but really youre rather trying on more commonplace occasions.

HIGGINS. Am I? Very sorry. [*Beaming suddenly*] I suppose I am, you know. [*Uproariously*] Ha, ha!

MISS EYNSFORD HILL [*who considers Higgins quite eligible matrimonially*] I sympathize. *I* havnt any small talk. If people would only be frank and say what they really think!

HIGGINS [*relapsing into gloom*] Lord forbid!

MRS EYNSFORD HILL [*taking up her daughter's cue*] But why?

HIGGINS. What they think they ought to think is bad enough, Lord knows; but what they really think would break up the whole show. Do you suppose it would be really agreeable if I were to come out now with what *I* really think?

MISS EYNSFORD HILL [*gaily*] Is it so very cynical?

HIGGINS. Cynical! Who the dickens said it was cynical? I mean it wouldnt be decent.

MRS EYNSFORD HILL [*seriously*] Oh! I'm sure you dont mean that, Mr Higgins.

HIGGINS. You see, we're all savages, more or less. We're supposed to be civilized and cultured—to know all about poetry and philosophy and art and science, and so on; but how many of us know even the meanings of these names? [*To Miss Hill*] What do you know of poetry? [*To Mrs Hill*] What do you know of science? [*Indicating Freddy*] What does he know of art or science or anything else? What the devil do you imagine I know of philosophy?

MRS HIGGINS [*warningly*] Or of manners, Henry?

THE PARLOR-MAID [*opening the door*] Miss Doolittle. [*She withdraws*].

HIGGINS [*rising hastily and running to Mrs Higgins*] Here she is, mother. [*He stands on tiptoe and makes signs over his mother's head to Eliza to indicate to her which lady is her hostess*].

Eliza, who is exquisitely dressed, produces an impression of such remarkable distinction and beauty as she enters that they all rise, quite fluttered. Guided by Higgins's signals, she comes to Mrs Higgins with studied grace.

LIZA [*speaking with pedantic correctness of pronunciation and great beauty of tone*] How do you do, Mrs Higgins? [*She gasps slightly in making sure of the H in Higgins, but is quite successful*]. Mr Higgins told me I might come.

MRS HIGGINS [*cordially*] Quite right: I'm very glad indeed to see you.

PICKERING. How do you do, Miss Doolittle?

LIZA [*shaking hands with him*] Colonel Pickering, is it not?

MRS EYNSFORD HILL. I feel sure we have met before, Miss Doolittle. I remember your eyes.

LIZA. How do you do? [*She sits down on the ottoman gracefully in the place just left vacant by Higgins*].

MRS EYNSFORD HILL [*introducing*] My daughter Clara.

LIZA. How do you do?

CLARA [*impulsively*] How do you do? [*She sits down on the ottoman beside Eliza, devouring her with her eyes*].

FREDDY [*coming to their side of the ottoman*] Ive certainly had the pleasure.

MRS EYNSFORD HILL [*introducing*] My son Freddy.

LIZA. How do you do?

Freddy bows and sits down in the Elizabethan chair, infatuated.

HIGGINS [*suddenly*] By George, yes: it all comes back to me!

57

[*They stare at him*]. Covent Garden! [*Lamentably*] What a damned thing!

MRS HIGGINS. Henry, please! [*He is about to sit on the edge of the table*] Dont sit on my writing-table: youll break it.

HIGGINS [*sulkily*] Sorry.

He goes to the divan, stumbling into the fender and over the fire-irons on his way; extricating himself with muttered imprecations; and finishing his disastrous journey by throwing himself so impatiently on the divan that he almost breaks it. Mrs Higgins looks at him, but controls herself and says nothing.

A long and painful pause ensues.

MRS HIGGINS [*at last, conversationally*] Will it rain, do you think?

LIZA. The shallow depression in the west of these islands is likely to move slowly in an easterly direction. There are no indications of any great change in the barometrical situation.

FREDDY. Ha! ha! how awfully funny!

LIZA. What is wrong with that, young man? I bet I got it right.

FREDDY. Killing!

MRS EYNSFORD HILL. I'm sure I hope it wont turn cold. Theres so much influenza about. It runs right through our whole family regularly every spring.

LIZA [*darkly*] My aunt died of influenza: so they said.

MRS EYNSFORD HILL [*clicks her tongue sympathetically*]!!!

LIZA [*in the same tragic tone*] But it's my belief they done the old woman in.

MRS HIGGINS [*puzzled*] Done her in?

LIZA. Y-e-e-e-es, Lord love you! Why should she die of influenza? She come through diphtheria right enough the year before. I saw her with my own eyes. Fairly blue with it, she was. They all thought she was dead; but my father he kept ladling gin down her throat til she came to so sudden that she bit the bowl off the spoon.

MRS EYNSFORD HILL [*startled*] Dear me!

PYGMALION

LIZA [*piling up the indictment*] What call would a woman with that strength in her have to die of influenza? What become of her new straw hat that should have come to me? Somebody pinched it; and what I say is, them as pinched it done her in.

MRS EYNSFORD HILL. What does doing her in mean?

HIGGINS [*hastily*] Oh, thats the new small talk. To do a person in means to kill them.

MRS EYNSFORD HILL [*to Eliza, horrified*] You surely dont believe that your aunt was killed?

LIZA. Do I not! Them she lived with would have killed her for a hat-pin, let alone a hat.

MRS EYNSFORD HILL. But it cant have been right for your father to pour spirits down her throat like that. It might have killed her.

LIZA. Not her. Gin was mother's milk to her. Besides, he'd poured so much down his own throat that he knew the good of it.

MRS EYNSFORD HILL. Do you mean that he drank?

LIZA. Drank! My word! Something chronic.

MRS EYNSFORD HILL. How dreadful for you!

LIZA. Not a bit. It never did him no harm what I could see. But then he did not keep it up regular. [*Cheerfully*] On the burst, as you might say, from time to time. And always more agreeable when he had a drop in. When he was out of work, my mother used to give him fourpence and tell him to go out and not come back until he'd drunk himself cheerful and loving-like. Theres lots of women has to make their husbands drunk to make them fit to live with. [*Now quite at her ease*] You see, it's like this. If a man has a bit of a conscience, it always takes him when he's sober; and then it makes him low-spirited. A drop of booze just takes that off and makes him happy. [*To Freddy, who is in convulsions of suppressed laughter*] Here! what are you sniggering at?

FREDDY. The new small talk. You do it so awfully well.

LIZA. If I was doing it proper, what was you laughing at? [*To Higgins*] Have I said anything I oughtnt?

59

MRS HIGGINS [*interposing*] Not at all, Miss Doolittle.

LIZA. Well, thats a mercy, anyhow. [*Expansively*] What I always say is—

HIGGINS [*rising and looking at his watch*] Ahem!

LIZA [*looking round at him; taking the hint; and rising*] Well: I must go. [*They all rise. Freddy goes to the door*]. So pleased to have met you. Goodbye. [*She shakes hands with Mrs Higgins*].

MRS HIGGINS. Goodbye.

LIZA. Goodbye, Colonel Pickering.

PICKERING. Goodbye, Miss Doolittle. [*They shake hands*].

LIZA [*nodding to the others*] Goodbye, all.

FREDDY [*opening the door for her*] Are you walking across the Park, Miss Doolittle? If so—

LIZA [*with perfectly elegant diction*] Walk! Not bloody likely. [*Sensation*]. I am going in a taxi. [*She goes out*].

Pickering gasps and sits down. Freddy goes out on the balcony to catch another glimpse of Eliza.

MRS EYNSFORD HILL [*suffering from shock*] Well, I really cant get used to the new ways.

CLARA [*throwing herself discontentedly into the Elizabethan chair*] Oh, it's all right, mamma, quite right. People will think we never go anywhere or see anybody if you are so old-fashioned.

MRS EYNSFORD HILL. I daresay I am very old-fashioned; but I do hope you wont begin using that expression, Clara. I have got accustomed to hear you talking about men as rotters, and calling everything filthy and beastly; though I do think it horrible and unladylike. But this last is really too much. Dont you think so, Colonel Pickering?

PICKERING. Dont ask me. Ive been away in India for several years; and manners have changed so much that I sometimes dont know whether I'm at a respectable dinner-table or in a ship's forecastle.

CLARA. It's all a matter of habit. Theres no right or wrong in it. Nobody means anything by it. And it's so quaint, and gives such a smart emphasis to things that are not in themselves very witty. I find the new small talk delightful and quite innocent.

MRS EYNSFORD HILL [*rising*] Well, after that, I think it's time for us to go.

Pickering and Higgins rise.

CLARA [*rising*] Oh yes: we have three at-homes to go to still. Goodbye, Mrs Higgins. Goodbye, Colonel Pickering. Goodbye, Professor Higgins.

HIGGINS [*coming grimly at her from the divan, and accompanying her to the door*] Goodbye. Be sure you try on that small talk at the three at-homes. Dont be nerv ⌐us about it. Pitch it in strong.

CLARA [*all smiles*] I will. Goodbye. Such nonsense, all this early Victorian prudery!

HIGGINS [*tempting her*] Such damned nonsense!

CLARA. Such bloody nonsense!

MRS EYNSFORD HILL [*convulsively*] Clara!

CLARA. Ha! ha! [*She goes out radiant, conscious of being thoroughly up to date, and is heard descending the stairs in a stream of silvery laughter*].

FREDDY [*to the heavens at large*] Well, I ask you— [*He gives it up, and comes to Mrs Higgins*]. Goodbye.

MRS HIGGINS [*shaking hands*] Goodbye. Would you like to meet Miss Doolittle again?

FREDDY [*eagerly*] Yes, I should, most awfully.

MRS HIGGINS. Well, you know my days.

FREDDY. Yes, Thanks awfully. Goodbye. [*He goes out*].

MRS EYNSFORD HILL. Goodbye, Mr Higgins.

HIGGINS. Goodbye. Goodbye.

MRS EYNSFORD HILL [*to Pickering*] It's no use. I shall never be able to bring myself to use that word.

PICKERING. Dont. It's not compulsory, you know. Youll get on quite well without it.

MRS EYNSFORD HILL. Only, Clara is so down on me if I am not positively reeking with the latest slang. Goodbye.

PICKERING. Goodbye [*They shake hands*].

MRS EYNSFORD HILL [*to Mrs Higgins*] You mustnt mind Clara. [*Pickering, catching from her lowered tone that this is not meant for him to hear, discreetly joins Higgins at the window*]. We're so poor! and she gets so few parties, poor child! She doesnt quite know. [*Mrs Higgins, seeing that her eyes are moist, takes her hand sympathetically and goes with her to the door*]. But the boy is nice. Dont you think so?

MRS HIGGINS. Oh, quite nice. I shall always be delighted to see him.

MRS EYNSFORD HILL. Thank you, dear. Goodbye. [*She goes out*].

HIGGINS [*eagerly*] Well? Is Eliza presentable [*he swoops on his mother and drags her to the ottoman, where she sits down in Eliza's place with her son on her left*]?

Pickering returns to his chair on her right.

MRS HIGGINS. You silly boy, of course she's not presentable. She's a triumph of your art and of her dressmaker's; but if you suppose for a moment that she doesnt give herself away in every sentence she utters, you must be perfectly cracked about her.

PICKERING. But dont you think something might be done? I mean something to eliminate the sanguinary element from her conversation.

MRS HIGGINS. Not as long as she is in Henry's hands.

HIGGINS [*aggrieved*] Do you mean that my language is improper?

MRS HIGGINS. No, dearest: it would be quite proper—say on a canal barge; but it would not be proper for her at a garden party.

HIGGINS [*deeply injured*] Well I must say—

PICKERING [*interrupting him*] Come, Higgins: you must learn to know yourself. I havnt heard such language as yours since we used to review the volunteers in Hyde Park twenty years ago.

HIGGINS [*sulkily*] Oh, well, if you say so, I suppose I dont always talk like a bishop.

PYGMALION

MRS HIGGINS [*quieting Henry with a touch*] Colonel Pickering: will you tell me what is the exact state of things in Wimpole Street?

PICKERING [*cheerfully: as if this completely changed the subject*] Well, I have come to live there with Henry. We work together at my Indian Dialects; and we think it more convenient—

MRS HIGGINS. Quite so. I know all about that: it's an excellent arrangement. But where does this girl live?

HIGGINS. With us, of course. Where should she live?

MRS HIGGINS. But on what terms? Is she a servant? If not, what is she?

PICKERING [*slowly*] I think I know what you mean, Mrs Higgins.

HIGGINS. Well, dash me if *I* do! Ive had to work at the girl every day for months to get her to her present pitch. Besides, she's useful. She knows where my things are, and remembers my appointments and so forth.

MRS HIGGINS. How does your housekeeper get on with her?

HIGGINS. Mrs Pearce? Oh, she's jolly glad to get so much taken off her hands; for before Eliza came, she used to have to find things and remind me of my appointments. But she's got some silly bee in her bonnet about Eliza. She keeps saying "You dont think, sir": doesnt she, Pick?

PICKERING. Yes: thats the formula. "You dont think, sir." Thats the end of every conversation about Eliza.

HIGGINS. As if I ever stop thinking about the girl and her confounded vowels and consonants. I'm worn out, thinking about her, and watching her lips and her teeth and her tongue, not to mention her soul, which is the quaintest of the lot.

MRS HIGGINS. You certainly are a pretty pair of babies, playing with your live doll.

HIGGINS. Playing! The hardest job I ever tackled: make no mistake about that, mother. But you have no idea how frightfully interesting it is to take a human being and change her into a quite different human being by creating a new speech for her. It's filling up the deepest gulf that separates class from class and soul from soul.

PICKERING [*drawing his chair closer to Mrs Higgins and bending over to her eagerly*] Yes: it's enormously interesting. I assure you, Mrs Higgins, we take Eliza very seriously. Every week—every day almost—there is some new change. [*Closer again*] We keep records of every stage—dozens of gramophone disks and photographs—

HIGGINS [*assailing her at the other ear*] Yes, by George: it's the most absorbing experiment I ever tackled. She regularly fills our lives up: doesnt she, Pick?

PICKERING. We're always talking Eliza.

HIGGINS. Teaching Eliza.

PICKERING. Dressing Eliza.

MRS HIGGINS. What!

HIGGINS. Inventing new Elizas.

HIGGINS.	[*speaking together*]	You know, she has the most extraordinary quickness of ear:
PICKERING.		I assure you, my dear Mrs Higgins, that girl
HIGGINS.		just like a parrot. Ive tried her with every
PICKERING.		is a genius. She can play the piano quite beautifully.
HIGGINS.		possible sort of sound that a human being can make—
PICKERING.		We have taken her to classical concerts and to music
HIGGINS.		Continental dialects, African dialects, Hottentot
PICKERING.		halls; and it's all the same to her: she plays everything

PYGMALION

HIGGINS.		clicks, things it took me years to get
	[speaking	hold of; and
PICKERING.	*together]*	she hears right off when she comes home, whether it's
HIGGINS.		she picks them up like a shot, right away, as if she had
PICKERING.		Beethoven and Brahms or Lehar and Lionel Monckton;
HIGGINS.		been at it all her life.
PICKERING.		though six months ago, she'd never as much as touched a piano—

MRS HIGGINS [*putting her fingers in her ears, as they are by this time shouting one another down with an intolerable noise*] Sh-sh-sh—sh! [*They stop*].

PICKERING. I beg your pardon. [*He draws his chair back apologetically*].

HIGGINS. Sorry. When Pickering starts shouting nobody can get a word in edgeways.

MRS HIGGINS. Be quiet, Henry. Colonel Pickering: dont you realize that when Eliza walked into Wimpole Street, something walked in with her?

PICKERING. Her father did. But Henry soon got rid of him.

MRS HIGGINS. It would have been more to the point if her mother had. But as her mother didnt something else did.

PICKERING. But what?

MRS HIGGINS [*unconsciously dating herself by the word*] A problem.

PICKERING. Oh, I see. The problem of how to pass her off as a lady.

HIGGINS. I'll solve that problem. Ive half solved it already.

MRS HIGGINS. No, you two infinitely stupid male creatures: the problem of what is to be done with her afterwards.

HIGGINS. I dont see anything in that. She can go her own way, with all the advantages I have given her.

PYGMALION

MRS HIGGINS. The advantages of that poor woman who was here just now! The manners and habits that disqualify a fine lady from earning her own living without giving her a fine lady's income! Is that what you mean?

PICKERING [*indulgently, being rather bored*] Oh, that will be all right, Mrs Higgins. [*He rises to go*].

HIGGINS [*rising also*] We'll find her some light employment.

PICKERING. She's happy enough. Dont you worry about her. Goodbye. [*He shakes hands as if he were consoling a frightened child, and makes for the door*].

HIGGINS. Anyhow, theres no good bothering now. The thing's done. Goodbye, mother. [*He kisses her, and follows Pickering*].

PICKERING [*turning for a final consolation*] There are plenty of openings. We'll do whats right. Goodbye.

HIGGINS [*to Pickering as they go out together*] Lets take her to the Shakespear exhibition at Earls Court.

PICKERING. Yes: lets. Her remarks will be delicious.

HIGGINS. She'll mimic all the people for us when we get home.

PICKERING. Ripping. [*Both are heard laughing as they go downstairs*].

MRS HIGGINS [*rises with an impatient bounce, and returns to her work at the writing-table. She sweeps a litter of disarranged papers out of her way; snatches a sheet of paper from her stationery case; and tries resolutely to write. At the third line she gives it up; flings down her pen; grips the table angrily and exclaims*] Oh, men! men!! men!!!

* * * * * *

Clearly Eliza will not pass as a duchess yet; and Higgins's bet remains unwon. But the six months are not yet exhausted; and just in time Eliza does actually pass as a princess. For a glimpse of how she did it imagine an Embassy in London one summer evening after dark. The hall door has an awning and a carpet across the sidewalk to the kerb, because a grand reception is in progress. A small crowd is lined up to see the guests arrive.

66

PYGMALION

A Rolls-Royce car drives up. Pickering in evening dress, with medals and orders, alights, and hands out Eliza, in opera cloak, evening dress, diamonds, fan, flowers and all accessories. Higgins follows. The car drives off; and the three go up the steps and into the house, the door opening for them as they approach.

Inside the house they find themselves in a spacious hall from which the grand staircase rises. On the left are the arrangements for the gentlemen's cloaks. The male guests are depositing their hats and wraps there.

On the right is a door leading to the ladies' cloakroom. Ladies are going in cloaked and coming out in splendor. Pickering whispers to Eliza and points out the ladies' room. She goes into it. Higgins and Pickering take off their overcoats and take tickets for them from the attendant.

One of the guests, occupied in the same way, has his back turned. Having taken his ticket, he turns round and reveals himself as an important looking young man with an astonishingly hairy face. He has an enormous moustache, flowing out into luxuriant whiskers. Waves of hair cluster on his brow. His hair is cropped closely at the back, and glows with oil. Otherwise he is very smart. He wears several worthless orders. He is evidently a foreigner, guessable as a whiskered Pandour from Hungary; but in spite of the ferocity of his moustache he is amiable and genially voluble.

Recognizing Higgins, he flings his arms wide apart and approaches him enthusiastically.

WHISKERS. Maestro, maestro [*he embraces Higgins and kisses him on both cheeks*]. You remember me?

HIGGINS. No I dont. Who the devil are you?

WHISKERS. I am your pupil: your first pupil, your best and greatest pupil. I am little Nepommuck, the marvellous boy. I have made your name famous throughout Europe. You teach me phonetic. You cannot forget ME.

HIGGINS. Why dont you shave?

NEPOMMUCK. I have not your imposing appearance, your chin, your brow. Nobody notice me when I shave. Now I am famous: they call me Hairy Faced Dick.

HIGGINS. And what are you doing here among all these swells?

NEPOMMUCK. I am interpreter. I speak 32 languages. I am indispensable at these international parties. You are great cockney specialist: you place a man anywhere in London the moment he open his mouth. I place any man in Europe.

A footman hurries down the grand staircase and comes to Nepommuck.

FOOTMAN. You are wanted upstairs. Her Excellency cannot understand the Greek gentleman.

NEPOMMUCK. Thank you, yes, immediately.

The footman goes and is lost in the crowd.

NEPOMMUCK [*to Higgins*] This Greek diplomatist pretends he cannot speak nor understand English. He cannot deceive me. He is the son of a Clerkenwell watchmaker. He speaks English so villainously that he dare not utter a word of it without betraying his origin. I help him to pretend; but I make him pay through the nose. I make them all pay. Ha ha! [*He hurries upstairs*].

PICKERING. Is this fellow really an expert? Can he find out Eliza and blackmail her?

HIGGINS. We shall see. If he finds her out I lose my bet.

Eliza comes from the cloakroom and joins them.

PICKERING. Well, Eliza, now for it. Are you ready?

LIZA. Are you nervous, Colonel?

PICKERING. Frightfully. I feel exactly as I felt before my first battle. It's the first time that frightens.

LIZA. It is not the first time for me, Colonel. I have done this fifty times—hundreds of times—in my little piggery in Angel Court in my day-dreams. I am in a dream now. Promise me not to let Professor Higgins wake me; for if he does I shall forget everything and talk as I used to in Drury Lane.

PICKERING. Not a word, Higgins. [*To Eliza*] Now, ready?

LIZA. Ready.

PICKERING. Go.

They mount the stairs, Higgins last. Pickering whispers to the footman on the first landing.

FIRST LANDING FOOTMAN. Miss Doolittle, Colonel Pickering, Professor Higgins.

SECOND LANDING FOOTMAN. Miss Doolittle, Colonel Pickering, Professor Higgins.

At the top of the staircase the Ambassador and his wife, with Nepommuck at her elbow, are receiving.

HOSTESS [*taking Eliza's hand*] How d'ye do?

HOST [*same play*] How d'ye do? How d'ye do, Pickering?

LIZA [*with a beautiful gravity that awes her hostess*] How do you do? [*She passes on to the drawing room*].

HOSTESS. Is that your adopted daughter, Colonel Pickering? She will make a sensation.

PICKERING. Most kind of you to invite her for me. [*He passes on*].

HOSTESS [*to Nepommuck*] Find out all about her.

NEPOMMUCK [*bowing*] Excellency—[*he goes into the crowd*].

HOST. How d'ye do, Higgins? You have a rival here tonight. He introduced himself as your pupil. Is he any good?

HIGGINS. He can learn a language in a fortnight—knows dozens of them. A sure mark of a fool. As a phonetician, no good whatever.

HOSTESS. How d'ye do, Professor?

HIGGINS. How do you do? Fearful bore for you this sort of thing. Forgive my part in it. [*He passes on*].

In the drawing room and its suite of salons the reception is in full swing. Eliza passes through. She is so intent on her ordeal that she walks like a somnambulist in a desert instead of a débutante in a fashionable crowd. They stop talking to look at her, admiring her dress, her jewels, and her strangely attractive self. Some of the younger ones at the back stand on their chairs to see.

The Host and Hostess come in from the staircase and mingle with their guests. Higgins, gloomy and contemptuous of the whole business, comes into the group where they are chatting.

HOSTESS. Ah, here is Professor Higgins: he will tell us. Tell us all about the wonderful young lady, Professor.

HIGGINS [*almost morosely*] What wonderful young lady?

HOSTESS. You know very well. They tell me there has been nothing like her in London since people stood on their chairs to look at Mrs Langtry.

Nepommuck joins the group, full of news.

HOSTESS. Ah, here you are at last, Nepommuck. Have you found out all about the Doolittle lady?

NEPOMMUCK. I have found out all about her. She is a fraud.

HOSTESS. A fraud! Oh no.

NEPOMMUCK. YES, yes. She cannot deceive me. Her name cannot be Doolittle.

HIGGINS. Why?

NEPOMMUCK. Because Doolittle is an English name. And she is not English.

HOSTESS. Oh, nonsense! She speaks English perfectly.

NEPOMMUCK. Too perfectly. Can you shew me any English woman who speaks English as it should be spoken? Only foreigners who have been taught to speak it speak it well.

HOSTESS. Certainly she terrified me by the way she said How d'ye do. I had a schoolmistress who talked like that; and I was mortally afraid of her. But if she is not English what is she?

NEPOMMUCK. Hungarian.

ALL THE REST. Hungarian!

NEPOMMUCK. Hungarian. And of royal blood. I am Hungarian. My blood is royal.

HIGGINS. Did you speak to her in Hungarian?

NEPOMMUCK. I did. She was very clever. She said 'Please speak to me in English: I do not understand French." French!

She pretend not to know the difference between Hungarian and French. Impossible: she knows both.

HIGGINS. And the blood royal? How did you find that out?

NEPOMMUCK. Instinct, maestro, instinct. Only the Magyar races can produce that air of the divine right, those resolute eyes. She is a princess.

HOST. What do you say, Professor?

HIGGINS. I say an ordinary London girl out of the gutter and taught to speak by an expert. I place her in Drury Lane.

NEPOMMUCK. Ha ha ha! Oh, maestro, maestro, you are mad on the subject of cockney dialects. The London gutter is the whole world for you.

HIGGINS [to the Hostess] What does your Excellency say?

HOSTESS. Oh, of course I agree with Nepommuck. She must be a princess at least.

HOST. Not necessarily legitimate, of course. Morganatic perhaps. But that is undoubtedly her class.

HIGGINS. I stick to my opinion.

HOSTESS. Oh, you are incorrigible.

The group breaks up, leaving Higgins isolated. Pickering joins him.

PICKERING. Where is Eliza? We must keep an eye on her.

Eliza joins them.

LIZA. I dont think I can bear much more. The people all stare so at me. An old lady has just told me that I speak exactly like Queen Victoria. I am sorry if I have lost your bet. I have done my best; but nothing can make me the same as these people.

PICKERING. You have not lost it, my dear. You have won it ten times over.

HIGGINS. Let us get out of this. I have had enough of chattering to these fools.

PICKERING. Eliza is tired; and I am hungry. Let us clear out and have supper somewhere.

ACT IV

The Wimpole Street laboratory. Midnight. Nobody in the room. The clock on the mantelpiece strikes twelve. The fire is not alight: it is a summer night.

Presently Higgins and Pickering are heard on the stairs.

HIGGINS [*calling down to Pickering*] I say, Pick: lock up, will you? I shant be going out again.

PICKERING. Right. Can Mrs Pearce go to bed? We dont want anything more, do we?

HIGGINS. Lord, no!

Eliza opens the door and is seen on the lighted landing in all the finery in which she has just won Higgins's bet for him. She comes to the hearth, and switches on the electric lights there. She is tired: her pallor contrasts strongly with her dark eyes and hair; and her expression is almost tragic. She takes off her cloak; puts her fan and gloves on the piano; and sits down on the bench, brooding and silent. Higgins, in evening dress, with overcoat and hat, comes in, carrying a smoking jacket which he has picked up downstairs. He takes off the hat and overcoat; throws them carelessly on the newspaper stand; disposes of his coat in the same way; puts on the smoking jacket; and throws himself wearily into the easy-chair at the hearth. Pickering, similarly attired, comes in. He also takes off his hat and overcoat, and is about to throw them on Higgins's when he hesitates.

PICKERING. I say: Mrs Pearce will row if we leave these things lying about in the drawing room.

HIGGINS. Oh, chuck them over the bannisters into the hall. She'll find them there in the morning and put them away all right. She'll think we were drunk.

PICKERING. We are, slightly. Are there any letters?

HIGGINS. I didnt look. [*Pickering takes the overcoats and hats and goes downstairs. Higgins begins half singing half yawning an air from La Fanciulla del Golden West. Suddenly he stops and exclaims*]

I wonder where the devil my slippers are!

Eliza looks at him darkly; then rises suddenly and leaves the room.
Higgins yawns again, and resumes his song.

Pickering returns, with the contents of the letter-box in his hand.

PICKERING. Only circulars, and this coroneted billet-doux for you. [*He throws the circulars into the fender, and posts himself on the hearthrug, with his back to the grate*].

HIGGINS [*glancing at the billet-doux*] Money-lender. [*He throws the letter after the circulars*].

Eliza returns with a pair of large down-at-heel slippers. She places them on the carpet before Higgins, and sits as before without a word.

HIGGINS [*yawning again*] Oh Lord! What an evening! What a crew! What a silly tomfoolery! [*He raises his shoe to unlace it, and catches sight of the slippers. He stops unlacing and looks at them as if they had appeared there of their own accord*]. Oh! theyre there, are they?

PICKERING [*stretching himself*] Well, I feel a bit tired. It's been a long day. The garden party, a dinner party, and the reception! Rather too much of a good thing. But youve won your bet, Higgins. Eliza did the trick, and something to spare, eh?

HIGGINS [*fervently*] Thank God it's over!

Eliza flinches violently; but they take no notice of her; and she recovers herself and sits stonily as before.

PICKERING. Were you nervous at the garden party? *I* was. Eliza didnt seem a bit nervous.

HIGGINS. Oh, she wasnt nervous. I knew she'd be all right. No: it's the strain of putting the job through all these months that has told on me. It was interesting enough at first, while we were at the phonetics; but after that I got deadly sick of it. If I hadnt backed myself to do it I should have chucked the whole thing up two months ago. It was a silly notion: the whole thing has been a bore.

PICKERING. Oh come! the garden party was frightfully exciting. My heart began beating like anything.

HIGGINS. Yes, for the first three minutes. But when I saw we were going to win hands down, I felt like a bear in a cage, hanging about doing nothing. The dinner was worse: sitting gorging there for over an hour, with nobody but a damned fool of a fashionable woman to talk to! I tell you, Pickering, never again for me. No more artificial duchesses. The whole thing has been simple purgatory.

PICKERING. Youve never been broken in properly to the social routine. [*Strolling over to the piano*] I rather enjoy dipping into it occasionally myself: it makes me feel young again. Anyhow, it was a great success: an immense success. I was quite frightened once or twice because Eliza was doing it so well. You see, lots of the real people cant do it at all: theyre such fools that they think style comes by nature to people in their position; and so they never learn. Theres always something professional about doing a thing superlatively well.

HIGGINS. Yes: thats what drives me mad: the silly people dont know their own silly business. [*Rising*] However, it's over and done with; and now I can go to bed at last without dreading tomorrow.

Eliza's beauty becomes murderous.

PICKERING. I think I shall turn in too. Still, it's been a great occasion: a triumph for you. Goodnight. [*He goes*].

HIGGINS [*following him*] Goodnight. [*Over his shoulder, at the door*] Put out the lights, Eliza; and tell Mrs Pearce not to make coffee for me in the morning: I'll take tea. [*He goes out*].

Eliza tries to control herself and feel indifferent as she rises and walks across to the hearth to switch off the lights. By the time she gets there she is on the point of screaming. She sits down in Higgins's chair and holds on hard to the arms. Finally she gives way and flings herself furiously on the floor, raging.

HIGGINS [*in despairing wrath outside*] What the devil have I done with my slippers? [*He appears at the door*].

LIZA [*snatching up the slippers, and hurling them at him one after the other with all her force*] There are your slippers. And there. Take your slippers; and may you never have a day's luck with them!

HIGGINS [*astounded*] What on earth—! [*He comes to her*]. Whats the matter? Get up. [*He pulls her up*]. Anything wrong?

LIZA [*breathless*] Nothing wrong—with y o u. Ive won your bet for you, havnt I? Thats enough for you. *I* dont matter, I suppose.

HIGGINS. Y o u won my bet! You! Presumptuous insect! *I* won it. What did you throw those slippers at me for?

LIZA. Because I wanted to smash your face. I'd like to kill you, you selfish brute. Why didnt you leave me where you picked me out of—in the gutter? You thank God it's all over, and that now you can throw me back again there, do you? [*She crisps her fingers frantically*].

HIGGINS [*looking at her in cool wonder*] The creature is nervous, after all.

LIZA [*gives a suffocated scream of fury, and instinctively darts her nails at his face*]!!

HIGGINS [*catching her wrists*] Ah! would you? Claws in, you cat. How dare you shew your temper to me? Sit down and be quiet. [*He throws her roughly into the easy-chair*].

LIZA [*crushed by superior strength and weight*] Whats to become of me? Whats to become of me?

HIGGINS. How the devil do I know whats to become of you? What does it matter what becomes of you?

LIZA. You dont care. I know you dont care. You wouldnt care if I was dead. I'm nothing to you—not so much as them slippers.

HIGGINS [*thundering*] Those slippers.

LIZA [*with bitter submission*] Those slippers. I didnt think it made any difference now.

A pause. Eliza hopeless and crushed. Higgins a little uneasy.

HIGGINS [*in his loftiest manner*] Why have you begun going on like this? May I ask whether you complain of your treatment here?

LIZA. No.

PYGMALION

HIGGINS. Has anybody behaved badly to you? Colonel Pickering? Mrs Pearce? Any of the servants?

LIZA. No.

HIGGINS. I presume you dont pretend that *I* have treated you badly?

LIZA. No.

HIGGINS. I am glad to hear it. [*He moderates his tone*]. Perhaps youre tired after the strain of the day. Will you have a glass of champagne? [*He moves towards the door*].

LIZA. No. [*Recollecting her manners*] Thank you.

HIGGINS [*good-humored again*] This has been coming on you for some days. I suppose it was natural for you to be anxious about the garden party. But thats all over now. [*He pats her kindly on the shoulder. She writhes*]. Theres nothing more to worry about.

LIZA. No. Nothing more for y o u to worry about. [*She suddenly rises and gets away from him by going to the piano bench, where she sits and hides her face*]. Oh God! I wish I was dead.

HIGGINS [*staring after her in sincere surprise*] Why? In heaven's name, why? [*Reasonably, going to her*] Listen to me, Eliza. All this irritation is purely subjective.

LIZA. I dont understand. I'm too ignorant.

HIGGINS. It's only imagination. Low spirits and nothing else. Nobody's hurting you. Nothing's wrong. You go to bed like a good girl and sleep it off. Have a little cry and say your prayers: that will make you comfortable.

LIZA. I heard y o u r prayers. "Thank God it's all over!"

HIGGINS [*impatiently*] Well, dont y o u thank God it's all over? Now you are free and can do what you like.

LIZA [*pulling herself together in desperation*] What am I fit for? What have you left me fit for? Where am I to go? What am I to do? Whats to become of me?

HIGGINS [*enlightened, but not at all impressed*] Oh, tha t s whats worrying you, is it? [*He thrusts his hands into his pockets, and walks about in his usual manner, rattling the contents of his pockets,*

76

as if condescending to a trivial subject out of pure kindness]. I shouldnt bother about it if I were you. I should imagine you wont have much difficulty in settling yourself somewhere or other, though I hadnt quite realized that you were going away. [*She looks quickly at him: he does not look at her, but examines the dessert stand on the piano and decides that he will eat an apple*]. You might marry, you know. [*He bites a large piece out of the apple and munches it noisily*]. You see, Eliza, all men are not confirmed old bachelors like me and the Colonel. Most men are the marrying sort (poor devils!); and youre not bad-looking: it's quite a pleasure to look at you sometimes—not now, of course, because youre crying and looking as ugly as the very devil; but when youre all right and quite yourself, youre what I should call attractive. That is, to the people in the marrying line, you understand. You go to bed and have a good nice rest; and then get up and look at yourself in the glass; and you wont feel so cheap.

Eliza again looks at him, speechless, and does not stir.

The look is quite lost on him: he eats his apple with a dreamy expression of happiness, as it is quite a good one.

HIGGINS [*a genial afterthought occurring to him*] I daresay my mother could find some chap or other who would do very well.

LIZA. We were above that at the corner of Tottenham Court Road.

HIGGINS [*waking up*] What do you mean?

LIZA. I sold flowers. I didnt sell myself. Now youve made a lady of me I'm not fit to sell anything else. I wish youd left me where you found me.

HIGGINS [*slinging the core of the apple decisively into the grate*] Tosh, Eliza. Dont you insult human relations by dragging all this cant about buying and selling into it. You neednt marry the fellow if you dont like him.

LIZA. What else am I to do?

HIGGINS. Oh, lots of things. What about your old idea of a florist's shop? Pickering could set you up in one: he has lots of money. [*Chuckling*] He'll have to pay for all those togs you have been wearing today; and that, with the hire of the jewellery, will make a big hole in two hundred pounds. Why, six months ago you would have thought it the millennium to have a flower shop of your own. Come! youll be all right. I must clear off to bed: I'm devilish sleepy. By the way, I came down for something: I forget what it was.

LIZA. Your slippers.

HIGGINS. Oh yes, of course. You shied them at me. [*He picks them up, and is going out when she rises and speaks to him*].

LIZA. Before you go, sir—

HIGGINS [*dropping the slippers in his surprise at her calling him Sir*] Eh?

LIZA. Do my clothes belong to me or to Colonel Pickering?

HIGGINS [*coming back into the room as if her question were the very climax of unreason*] What the devil use would they be to Pickering?

LIZA. He might want them for the next girl you pick up to experiment on.

HIGGINS [*shocked and hurt*] Is t h a t the way you feel towards us?

LIZA. I dont want to hear anything more about that. All I want to know is whether anything belongs to me My own clothes were burnt.

HIGGINS. But what does it matter? Why need you start bothering about that in the middle of the night?

LIZA. I want to know what I may take away with me. I dont want to be accused of stealing.

HIGGINS [*now deeply wounded*] Stealing! You shouldnt have said that, Eliza. That shews a want of feeling.

LIZA. I'm sorry. I'm only a common ignorant girl; and in my station I have to be careful. There cant be any feelings between the like of you and the like of me. Please will you tell me what belongs to me and what doesnt?

HIGGINS [*very sulky*] You may take the whole damned houseful if you like. Except the jewels. Theyre hired. Will that satisfy you? [*He turns on his heel and is about to go in extreme dudgeon*].

LIZA [*drinking in his emotion like nectar, and nagging him to provoke a further supply*] Stop, please. [*She takes off her jewels*]. Will you take these to your room and keep them safe? I dont want to run the risk of their being missing.

HIGGINS [*furious*] Hand them over. [*She puts them into his hands*]. If these belonged to me instead of to the jeweller, I'd ram them down your ungrateful throat. [*He perfunctorily thrusts them into his pockets, unconsciously decorating himself with the protruding ends of the chains*].

LIZA [*taking a ring off*] This ring isnt the jeweller's: it's the one you bought me in Brighton. I dont want it now. [*Higgins dashes the ring violently into the fireplace, and turns on her so threateningly that she crouches over the piano with her hands over her face, and exclaims*] Dont you hit me.

HIGGINS. Hit you! You infamous creature, how dare you accuse me of such a thing? It is you who have hit me. You have wounded me to the heart.

LIZA [*thrilling with hidden joy*] I'm glad. Ive got a little of my own back, anyhow.

HIGGINS [*with dignity, in his finest professional style*] You have caused me to lose my temper: a thing that has hardly ever happened to me before. I prefer to say nothing more tonight. I am going to bed.

LIZA [*pertly*] Youd better leave a note for Mrs Pearce about the coffee; for she wont be told by me.

HIGGINS [*formally*] Damn Mrs Pearce; and damn the coffee; and damn you; and [*wildly*] damn my own folly in having lavished my hard-earned knowledge and the treasure of my regard and intimacy on a heartless guttersnipe. [*He goes out with impressive decorum, and spoils it by slamming the door savagely*].

Eliza goes down on her knees on the hearthrug to look for the ring. When she finds it she considers for a moment what to do with it.

Finally she flings it down on the dessert stand and goes upstairs in a tearing rage.

*   *   *   *   *   *

The furniture of Eliza's room has been increased by a big wardrobe and a sumptuous dressing-table. She comes in and switches on the electric light. She goes to the wardrobe; opens it; and pulls out a walking dress, a hat, and a pair of shoes, which she throws on the bed. She takes off her evening dress and shoes; then takes a padded hanger from the wardrobe; adjusts it carefully in the evening dress; and hangs it in the wardrobe, which she shuts with a slam. She puts on her walking shoes, her walking dress, and hat. She takes her wrist watch from the dressing-table and fastens it on. She pulls on her gloves; takes her vanity bag; and looks into it to see that her purse is there before hanging it on her wrist. She makes for the door. Every movement expresses her furious resolution.

She takes a last look at herself in the glass.

She suddenly puts out her tongue at herself; then leaves the room, switching off the electric light at the door.

Meanwhile, in the street outside, Freddy Eynsford Hill, lovelorn, is gazing up at the second floor, in which one of the windows is still lighted.

The light goes out.

FREDDY. Goodnight, darling, darling, darling.

Eliza comes out, giving the door a considerable bang behind her.

LIZA. Whatever are you doing here?

FREDDY. Nothing. I spend most of my nights here. It's the only place where I'm happy. Dont laugh at me, Miss Doolittle.

LIZA. Dont you call me Miss Doolittle, do you hear? Liza's good enough for me. [*She breaks down and grabs him by the shoulders*] Freddy: you dont think I'm a heartless guttersnipe, do you?

FREDDY. Oh no, no, darling: how can you imagine such a thing? You are the loveliest, dearest—

PYGMALION

He loses all self-control and smothers her with kisses. She, hungry for comfort, responds. They stand there in one another's arms.

An elderly police constable arrives.

CONSTABLE [*scandalized*] Now then! Now then!! Now then!!!

They release one another hastily.

FREDDY. Sorry, constable. Weve only just become engaged.

They run away.

The constable shakes his head, reflecting on his own courtship and on the vanity of human hopes. He moves off in the opposite direction with slow professional steps.

The flight of the lovers takes them to Cavendish Square. There they halt to consider their next move.

LIZA [*out of breath*] He didnt half give me a fright, that copper. But you answered him proper.

FREDDY. I hope I havnt taken you out of your way. Where were you going?

LIZA. To the river.

FREDDY. What for?

LIZA. To make a hole in it.

FREDDY [*horrified*] Eliza, darling. What do you mean? Whats the matter?

LIZA. Never mind. It doesnt matter now. Theres nobody in the world now but you and me, is there?

FREDDY. Not a soul.

They indulge in another embrace, and are again surprised by a much younger constable.

SECOND CONSTABLE. Now then, you two! Whats this? Where do you think you are? Move along here, double quick.

FREDDY. As you say, sir, double quick.

They run away again, and are in Hanover Square before they stop for another conference.

FREDDY. I had no idea the police were so devilishly prudish.

LIZA. It's their business to hunt girls off the streets.

PYGMALION

FREDDY. We must go somewhere. We cant wander about the streets all night.

LIZA. Cant we? I think it'd be lovely to wander about for ever.

FREDDY. Oh, darling.

They embrace again, oblivious of the arrival of a crawling taxi. It stops.

TAXIMAN. Can I drive you and the lady anywhere, sir?

They start asunder.

LIZA. Oh, Freddy, a taxi. The very thing.

FREDDY. But, damn it, I've no money.

LIZA. I have plenty. The Colonel thinks you should never go out without ten pounds in your pocket. Listen. We'll drive about all night; and in the morning I'll call on old Mrs Higgins and ask her what I ought to do. I'll tell you all about it in the cab. And the police wont touch us there.

FREDDY. Righto! Ripping. [*To the Taximan*] Wimbledon Common. [*They drive off*].

ACT V

Mrs Higgins's drawing room. She is at her writing-table as before. The parlor-maid comes in.

THE PARLOR-MAID [*at the door*] Mr Henry, maam, is downstairs with Colonel Pickering.

MRS HIGGINS. Well, shew them up.

THE PARLOR-MAID. Theyre using the telephone, maam. Telephoning to the police, I think.

MRS HIGGINS. What!

THE PARLOR-MAID [*coming further in and lowering her voice*] Mr Henry is in a state, maam. I thought I'd better tell you.

MRS HIGGINS. If you had told me that Mr Henry was not in a state it would have been more surprising. Tell them to come up when theyve finished with the police. I suppose he's lost something.

THE PARLOR-MAID. Yes, maam [*going*].

MRS HIGGINS. Go upstairs and tell Miss Doolittle that Mr Henry and the Colonel are here. Ask her not to come down til I send for her.

THE PARLOR-MAID. Yes, maam.

Higgins bursts in. He is, as the parlor-maid has said, in a state.

HIGGINS. Look here, mother: heres a confounded thing!

MRS HIGGINS. Yes, dear. Good morning. [*He checks his impatience and kisses her, whilst the parlor-maid goes out*]. What is it?

HIGGINS. Eliza's bolted.

MRS HIGGINS [*calmly continuing her writing*] You must have frightened her.

HIGGINS. Frightened her! nonsense! She was left last night, as usual, to turn out the lights and all that; and instead of going to bed she changed her clothes and went right off: her bed wasnt slept in. She came in a cab for her things before seven this morning; and that fool Mrs Pearce let her have them without telling me a word about it. What am I to do?

MRS HIGGINS. Do without, I'm afraid, Henry. The girl has a perfect right to leave if she chooses.

HIGGINS [*wandering distractedly across the room*] But I cant find anything. I dont know what appointments Ive got. I'm—[*Pickering comes in. Mrs Higgins puts down her pen and turns away from the writing-table*].

PICKERING [*shaking hands*] Good morning, Mrs Higgins. Has Henry told you? [*He sits down on the ottoman*].

HIGGINS. What does that ass of an inspector say? Have you offered a reward?

MRS HIGGINS [*rising in indignant amazement*] You dont mean to say you have set the police after Eliza.

HIGGINS. Of course. What are the police for? What else could we do? [*He sits in the Elizabethan chair*].

PICKERING. The inspector made a lot of difficulties. I really think he suspected us of some improper purpose.

MRS HIGGINS. Well, of course he did. What right have you to go to the police and give the girl's name as if she were a thief, or a lost umbrella, or something? Really! [*She sits down again, deeply vexed*].

HIGGINS. But we want to find her.

PICKERING. We cant let her go like this, you know, Mrs Higgins. What were we to do?

MRS HIGGINS. You have no more sense, either of you, than two children. Why—

The parlor-maid comes in and breaks off the conversation.

THE PARLOR-MAID. Mr Henry: a gentleman wants to see you very particular. He's been sent on from Wimpole Street.

HIGGINS. Oh, bother! I cant see anyone now. Who is it?

THE PARLOR-MAID. A Mr Doolittle, sir.

PICKERING. Doolittle! Do you mean the dustman?

THE PARLOR-MAID. Dustman! Oh no, sir: a gentleman.

HIGGINS [*springing up excitedly*] By George, Pick, it's some relative of hers that she's gone to. Somebody we know nothing about. [*To the parlor-maid*] Send him up, quick.

THE PARLOR-MAID. Yes, sir. [*She goes*].

HIGGINS [*eagerly, going to his mother*] Genteel relatives! now we shall hear something. [*He sits down in the Chippendale chair*].

MRS HIGGINS. Do you know any of her people?

PICKERING. Only her father: the fellow we told you about.

THE PARLOR-MAID [*announcing*] Mr Doolittle. [*She withdraws*].

Doolittle enters. He is resplendently dressed as for a fashionable wedding, and might, in fact, be the bridegroom. A flower in his buttonhole, a dazzling silk hat, and patent leather shoes complete the effect. He is too concerned with the business he has come on to notice Mrs Higgins. He walks straight to Higgins, and accosts him with vehement reproach.

DOOLITTLE [*indicating his own person*] See here! Do you see this? You done this.

HIGGINS. Done what, man?

DOOLITTLE. This, I tell you. Look at it. Look at this hat. Look at this coat.

PICKERING. Has Eliza been buying you clothes?

DOOLITTLE. Eliza! not she. Why would she buy me clothes?

MRS HIGGINS. Good morning, Mr Doolittle. Wont you sit down?

DOOLITTLE [*taken aback as he becomes conscious that he has forgotten his hostess*] Asking your pardon, maam. [*He approaches her and shakes her proffered hand*]. Thank you. [*He sits down on the ottoman, on Pickering's right*]. I am that full of what has happened to me that I cant think of anything else.

HIGGINS. What the dickens has happened to you?

DOOLITTLE. I shouldnt mind if it had only happened to me: anything might happen to anybody and nobody to blame but Providence, as you might say. But this is something that you done to me: yes, you, Enry Iggins.

HIGGINS. Have you found Eliza?

DOOLITTLE. Have you lost her?

HIGGINS. Yes.

DOOLITTLE. You have all the luck, you have. I aint found her; but she'll find me quick enough now after what you done to me.

MRS HIGGINS. But what has my son done to you, Mr Doolittle?

DOOLITTLE. Done to me! Ruined me. Destroyed my happiness. Tied me up and delivered me into the hands of middle class morality.

HIGGINS [rising intolerantly and standing over Doolittle] Youre raving. Youre drunk. Youre mad. I gave you five pounds. After that I had two conversations with you, at half-a-crown an hour. Ive never seen you since.

DOOLITTLE. Oh! Drunk am I? Mad am I? Tell me this. Did you or did you not write a letter to an old blighter in America that was giving five millions to found Moral Reform Societies all over the world, and that wanted you to invent a universal language for him?

HIGGINS. What! Ezra D. Wannafeller! He's dead. [He sits down again carelessly].

DOOLITTLE. Yes: he's dead; and I'm done for. Now did you or did you not write a letter to him to say that the most original moralist at present in England, to the best of your knowledge, was Alfred Doolittle, a common dustman?

HIGGINS. Oh, after your first visit I remember making some silly joke of the kind.

DOOLITTLE. Ah! you may well call it a silly joke. It put the lid on me right enough. Just give him the chance he wanted to shew that Americans is not like us: that they reckonize and respect merit in every class of life, however humble. Them words is in his blooming will, in which, Henry Higgins, thanks to your silly joking, he leaves me a share in his Pre-digested Cheese Trust worth three thousand a year on condition that I lecture for his

Wannafeller Moral Reform World League as often as they ask me up to six times a year.

HIGGINS. The devil he does! Whew! [*Brightening suddenly*] What a lark!

PICKERING. A safe thing for you, Doolittle. They wont ask you twice.

DOOLITTLE. It aint the lecturing I mind. I'll lecture them blue in the face, I will, and not turn a hair. It's making a gentleman of me that I object to. Who asked him to make a gentleman of me? I was happy. I was free. I touched pretty nigh everybody for money when I wanted it, same as I touched you, Enry Iggins. Now I am worrited; tied neck and heels; and everybody touches me for money. It's a fine thing for you, says my solicitor. Is it? says I. You mean it's a good thing for you, I says. When I was a poor man and had a solicitor once when they found a pram in the dust cart, he got me off, and got shut of me and got me shut of him as quick as he could. Same with the doctors: used to shove me out of the hospital before I could hardly stand on my legs, and nothing to pay. Now they finds out that I'm not a healthy man and cant live unless they looks after me twice a day. In the house I'm not let do a hand's turn for myself: somebody else must do it and touch me for it. A year ago I hadnt a relative in the world except two or three that wouldnt speak to me. Now Ive fifty, and not a decent week's wages among the lot of them. I have to live for others and not for myself: thats middle class morality. You talk of losing Eliza. Dont you be anxious: I bet she's on my doorstep by this: she that could support herself easy by selling flowers if I wasnt respectable. And the next one to touch me will be you, Enry Iggins. I'll have to learn to speak middle class language from you, instead of speaking proper English. Thats where youll come in; and I daresay thats what you done it for.

MRS HIGGINS. But, my dear Mr Doolittle, you need not suffer all this if you are really in earnest. Nobody can force you to

87

accept this bequest. You can repudiate it. Isnt that so, Colonel Pickering?

PICKERING. I believe so.

DOOLITTLE [*softening his manner in deference to her sex*] Thats the tragedy of it, maam. It's easy to say chuck it; but I havnt the nerve. Which of us has? We're all intimidated. Intimidated, maam: thats what we are. What is there for me if I chuck it but the workhouse in my old age? I have to dye my hair already to keep my job as a dustman. If I was one of the deserving poor, and had put by a bit, I could chuck it; but then why should I, acause the deserving poor might as well be millionaires for all the happiness they ever has. They dont know what happiness is. But I, as one of the undeserving poor, have nothing between me and the pauper's uniform but this here blasted three thousand a year that shoves me into the middle class. (Excuse the expression, maam; youd use it yourself if you had my provocation.) Theyve got you every way you turn: it's a choice between the Skilly of the workhouse and the Char Bydis of the middle class; and I havnt the nerve for the workhouse. Intimidated: thats what I am. Broke. Bought up. Happier men than me will call for my dust, and touch me for their tip; and I'll look on helpless, and envy them. And thats what your son has brought me to. [*He is overcome by emotion*].

MRS HIGGINS. Well, I'm very glad youre not going to do anything foolish, Mr Doolittle. For this solves the problem of Eliza's future. You can provide for her now.

DOOLITTLE [*with melancholy resignation*] Yes, maam: I'm expected to provide for everyone now, out of three thousand a year.

HIGGINS [*jumping up*] Nonsense! he cant provide for her. He shant provide for her. She doesnt belong to him. I paid him five pounds for her. Doolittle: either youre an honest man or a rogue.

DOOLITTLE [*tolerantly*] A little of both, Henry, like the rest of us: a little of both.

HIGGINS. Well, you took that money for the girl; and you have no right to take her as well.

MRS HIGGINS. Henry: dont be absurd. If you want to know where Eliza is, she is upstairs.

HIGGINS [amazed] Upstairs!!! Then I shall jolly soon fetch her downstairs. [He makes resolutely for the door].

MRS HIGGINS [rising and following him] Be quiet, Henry. Sit down.

HIGGINS. I—

MRS HIGGINS. Sit down, dear; and listen to me.

HIGGINS. Oh very well, very well, very well. [He throws himself ungraciously on the ottoman, with his face towards the windows]. But I think you might have told us this half an hour ago.

MRS HIGGINS. Eliza came to me this morning. She told me of the brutal way you two treated her.

HIGGINS [bounding up again] What!

PICKERING [rising also] My dear Mrs Higgins, she's been telling you stories. We didnt treat her brutally. We hardly said a word to her; and we parted on particularly good terms. [Turning on Higgins] Higgins: did you bully her after I went to bed?

HIGGINS. Just the other way about. She threw my slippers in my face. She behaved in the most outrageous way. I never gave her the slightest provocation. The slippers came bang into my face the moment I entered the room—before I had uttered a word. And used perfectly awful language.

PICKERING [astonished] But why? What did we do to her?

MRS HIGGINS. I think I know pretty well what you did. The girl is naturally rather affectionate, I think. Isnt she, Mr Doolittle?

DOOLITTLE. Very tender-hearted, maam. Takes after me.

MRS HIGGINS. Just so. She had become attached to you both. She worked very hard for you, Henry. I dont think you quite realize what anything in the nature of brain work means to a girl of her class. Well, it seems that when the great day of trial came, and she did this wonderful thing for you without making a single mistake, you two sat there and never said a word to her, but talked together of how glad you were that it was all over and how you had been bored with the whole thing. And then you were surprised because she threw your slippers at you! *I* should have thrown the fire-irons at you.

HIGGINS. We said nothing except that we were tired and wanted to go to bed. Did we, Pick?

PICKERING [*shrugging his shoulders*] That was all.

MRS HIGGINS [*ironically*] Quite sure?

PICKERING. Absolutely. Really, that was all.

MRS HIGGINS. You didnt thank her, or pet her, or admire her, or tell her how splendid she'd been.

HIGGINS [*impatiently*] But she knew all about that. We didnt make speeches to her, if thats what you mean.

PICKERING [*conscience stricken*] Perhaps we were a little inconsiderate. Is she very angry?

MRS HIGGINS [*returning to her place at the writing-table*] Well, I'm afraid she wont go back to Wimpole Street, especially now that Mr Doolittle is able to keep up the position you have thrust on her; but she says she is quite willing to meet you on friendly terms and to let bygones be bygones.

HIGGINS [*furious*] Is she, by George? Ho!

MRS HIGGINS. If you promise to behave yourself, Henry, I'll ask her to come down. If not, go home; for you have taken up quite enough of my time.

HIGGINS. Oh, all right. Very well, Pick: you behave yourself. Let us put on our best Sunday manners for this creature that we picked out of the mud. [*He flings himself sulkily into the Elizabethan chair*].

DOOLITTLE [*remonstrating*] Now, now, Enry Iggins! Have some consideration for my feelings as a middle class man.

MRS HIGGINS. Remember your promise, Henry. [*She presses the bell button on the writing-table*]. Mr Doolittle: will you be so good as to step out on the balcony for a moment. I dont want

Eliza to have the shock of your news until she has made it up with these two gentlemen. Would you mind?

DOOLITTLE. As you wish, lady. Anything to help Henry to keep her off my hands. [*He disappears through the window*].

The parlor-maid answers the bell. Pickering sits down in Doolittle's place.

MRS HIGGINS. Ask Miss Doolittle to come down, please.

THE PARLOR-MAID. Yes, maam. [*She goes out*].

MRS HIGGINS. Now, Henry: be good.

HIGGINS. I am behaving myself perfectly.

PICKERING. He is doing his best, Mrs Higgins.

A pause. Higgins throws back his head; stretches out his legs; and begins to whistle.

MRS HIGGINS. Henry, dearest, you dont look at all nice in that attitude.

HIGGINS [*pulling himself together*] I was not trying to look nice, mother.

MRS HIGGINS. It doesnt matter, dear. I only wanted to make you speak.

HIGGINS. Why?

MRS HIGGINS. Because you cant speak and whistle at the same time.

Higgins groans. Another very trying pause.

HIGGINS [*springing up, out of patience*] Where the devil is that girl? Are we to wait here all day?

Eliza enters, sunny, self-possessed, and giving a staggeringly convincing exhibition of ease of manner. She carries a little work-basket, and is very much at home. Pickering is too much taken aback to rise.

LIZA. How do you do, Professor Higgins? Are you quite well?

HIGGINS [*choking*] Am I— [*He can say no more*].

LIZA. But of course you are: you are never ill. So glad to see you again, Colonel Pickering. [*He rises hastily; and they shake hands*]. Quite chilly this morning, isnt it? [*She sits down on his left. He sits beside her*].

HIGGINS. Dont you dare try this game on me. I taught it to you; and it doesnt take me in. Get up and come home; and dont be a fool.

Eliza takes a piece of needlework from her basket, and begins to stitch at it, without taking the least notice of this outburst.

MRS HIGGINS. Very nicely put, indeed, Henry. No woman could resist such an invitation.

HIGGINS. You let her alone, mother. Let her speak for herself. You will jolly soon see whether she has an idea that I havnt put into her head or a word that I havnt put into her mouth. I tell you I have created this thing out of the squashed cabbage leaves of Covent Garden; and now she pretends to play the fine lady with me.

MRS HIGGINS [*placidly*] Yes, dear; but youll sit down, wont you?

Higgins sits down again, savagely.

LIZA [*to Pickering, taking no apparent notice of Higgins, and working away deftly*] Will you drop me altogether now that the experiment is over, Colonel Pickering?

PICKERING. Oh dont. You mustnt think of it as an experiment. It shocks me, somehow.

LIZA. Oh, I'm only a squashed cabbage leaf—

PICKERING [*impulsively*] No.

LIZA [*continuing quietly*] —but I owe so much to you that I should be very unhappy if you forgot me.

PICKERING. It's very kind of you to say so, Miss Doolittle.

LIZA. It's not because you paid for my dresses. I know you are generous to everybody with money. But it was from you that I learnt really nice manners; and that is what makes one a lady, isnt it? You see it was so very difficult for me with the example of Professor Higgins always before me. I was brought up to be just like him, unable to control myself, and using bad language on the slightest provocation. And I should never have known that ladies and gentlemen didnt behave like that if you hadnt been there.

HIGGINS. Well!!

PICKERING. Oh, thats only his way, you know. He doesnt mean it.

LIZA. Oh, *I* didnt mean it either, when I was a flower girl. It was only my way. But you see I did it; and thats what makes the difference after all.

PICKERING. No doubt. Still, he taught you to speak; and I couldnt have done that, you know.

LIZA [*trivially*] Of course: that is his profession.

HIGGINS. Damnation!

LIZA [*continuing*] It was just like learning to dance in the fashionable way: there was nothing more than that in it. But do you know what began my real education?

PICKERING. What?

LIZA [*stopping her work for a moment*] Your calling me Miss Doolittle that day when I first came to Wimpole Street. That was the beginning of self-respect for me. [*She resumes her stitching*]. And there were a hundred little things you never noticed, because they came naturally to you. Things about standing up and taking off your hat and opening doors—

PICKERING. Oh, that was nothing.

LIZA. Yes: things that shewed you thought and felt about me as if I were something better than a scullery-maid; though of course I know you would have been just the same to a scullery-maid if she had been let into the drawing room. You never took off your boots in the dining room when I was there.

PICKERING. You mustnt mind that. Higgins takes off his boots all over the place.

LIZA. I know. I am not blaming him. It is his way, isnt it? But it made such a difference to me that you didnt do it. You see, really and truly, apart from the things anyone can pick up (the dressing and the proper way of speaking, and so on), the difference between a lady and a flower girl is not how she behaves, but how she's treated. I shall always be a flower girl to Professor

Higgins, because he always treats me as a flower girl, and always will; but I know I can be a lady to you, because you always treat me as a lady, and always will.

MRS HIGGINS. Please dont grind your teeth, Henry.

PICKERING. Well, this is really very nice of you, Miss Doolittle.

LIZA. I should like you to call me Eliza, now, if you would.

PICKERING. Thank you. Eliza, of course.

LIZA. And I should like Professor Higgins to call me Miss Doolittle.

HIGGINS. I'll see you damned first.

MRS HIGGINS. Henry! Henry!

PICKERING [laughing] Why dont you slang back at him? Dont stand it. It would do him a lot of good.

LIZA. I cant. I could have done it once; but now I cant go back to it. You told me, you know, that when a child is brought to a foreign country, it picks up the language in a few weeks, and forgets its own. Well, I am a child in your country. I have forgotten my own language, and can speak nothing but yours. Thats the real break-off with the corner of Tottenham Court Road. Leaving Wimpole Street finishes it.

PICKERING [much alarmed] Oh! but youre coming back to Wimpole Street, arnt you? Youll forgive Higgins?

HIGGINS [rising] Forgive! Will she, by George! Let her go. Let her find out how she can get on without us. She will relapse into the gutter in three weeks without me at her elbow.

Doolittle appears at the centre window. With a look of dignified reproach at Higgins, he comes slowly and silently to his daughter, who, with her back to the window, is unconscious of his approach.

PICKERING. He's incorrigible, Eliza. You wont relapse, will you?

LIZA. No: not now. Never again. I have learnt my lesson. I dont believe I could utter one of the old sounds if I tried. [*Doolittle touches her on her left shoulder. She drops her work, losing her*

self-possession utterly at the spectacle of her father's splendor]
A-a-a-a-a-ah-ow-ooh!

HIGGINS [*with a crow of triumph*] Aha! Just so. A-a-a-a-ahowooh! A-a-a-a-ahowooh! A-a-a-a-ahowooh! Victory! Victory! [*He throws himself on the divan, folding his arms, and spraddling arrogantly*].

DOOLITTLE. Can you blame the girl? Dont look at me like that, Eliza. It aint my fault. Ive come into some money.

LIZA. You must have touched a millionaire this time, dad.

DOOLITTLE. I have. But I'm dressed something special today. I'm going to St George's, Hanover Square. Your stepmother is going to marry me.

LIZA [*angrily*] Youre going to let yourself down to marry that low common woman!

PICKERING [*quietly*] He ought to, Eliza. [*To Doolittle*] Why has she changed her mind?

DOOLITTLE [*sadly*] Intimidated, Governor. Intimidated. Middle class morality claims its victim. Wont you put on your hat, Liza, and come and see me turned off?

LIZA. If the Colonel says I must, I—I'll [*almost sobbing*] I'll demean myself. And get insulted for my pains, like enough.

DOOLITTLE. Dont be afraid: she never comes to words with anyone now, poor woman! respectability has broke all the spirit out of her.

PICKERING [*squeezing Eliza's elbow gently*] Be kind to them, Eliza. Make the best of it.

LIZA [*forcing a little smile for him through her vexation*] Oh well, just to shew theres no ill feeling. I'll be back in a moment. [*She goes out*].

DOOLITTLE [*sitting down beside Pickering*] I feel uncommon nervous about the ceremony, Colonel. I wish youd come and see me through it.

PICKERING. But youve been through it before, man. You were married to Eliza's mother.

DOOLITTLE. Who told you that, Colonel?

PICKERING. Well, nobody told me. But I concluded—naturally—

DOOLITTLE. No: that aint the natural way, Colonel: it's only the middle class way. My way was always the undeserving way. But dont say nothing to Eliza. She dont know: I always had a delicacy about telling her.

PICKERING. Quite right. We'll leave it so, if you dont mind.

DOOLITTLE. And youll come to the church, Colonel, and put me through straight?

PICKERING. With pleasure. As far as a bachelor can.

MRS HIGGINS. May I come, Mr Doolittle? I should be very sorry to miss your wedding.

DOOLITTLE. I should indeed be honored by your condescension, maam; and my poor old woman would take it as a tremenjous compliment. She's been very low, thinking of the happy days that are no more.

MRS HIGGINS [rising] I'll order the carriage and get ready. [The men rise, except Higgins]. I shant be more than fifteen minutes. [As she goes to the door Eliza comes in, hatted and buttoning her gloves]. I'm going to the church to see your father married, Eliza. You had better come in the brougham with me. Colonel Pickering can go on with the bridegroom.

Mrs Higgins goes out. Eliza comes to the middle of the room between the centre window and the ottoman. Pickering joins her.

DOOLITTLE. Bridegroom! What a word! It makes a man realize his position, somehow. [He takes up his hat and goes towards the door].

PICKERING. Before I go, Eliza, do forgive Higgins and come back to us.

LIZA. I dont think dad would allow me. Would you, dad?

DOOLITTLE [sad but magnanimous] They played you off very cunning, Eliza, them two sportsmen. If it had been only one of them, you could have nailed him. But you see, there was two;

and one of them chaperoned the other, as you might say. [*To Pickering*] It was artful of you, Colonel; but I bear no malice: I should have done the same myself. I been the victim of one woman after another all my life; and I dont grudge you two getting the better of Eliza. I shant interfere. It's time for us to go, Colonel. So long, Henry. See you in St George's, Eliza. [*He goes out*].

PICKERING [*coaxing*] Do stay with us, Eliza. [*He follows Doolittle*].

Eliza goes out on the balcony to avoid being alone with Higgins. He rises and joins her there. She immediately comes back into the room and makes for the door; but he goes along the balcony quickly and gets his back to the door before she reaches it.

HIGGINS. Well, Eliza, youve had a bit of your own back, as you call it. Have you had enough? and are you going to be reasonable? Or do you want any more?

LIZA. You want me back only to pick up your slippers and put up with your tempers and fetch and carry for you.

HIGGINS. I havnt said I wanted you back at all.

LIZA. Oh, indeed. Then what are we talking about?

HIGGINS. About you, not about me. If you come back I shall treat you just as I have always treated you. I cant change my nature; and I dont intend to change my manners. My manners are exactly the same as Colonel Pickering's.

LIZA. Thats not true. He treats a flower girl as if she was a duchess.

HIGGINS. And I treat a duchess as if she was a flower girl.

LIZA. I see. [*She turns away composedly, and sits on the ottoman, facing the window*]. The same to everybody.

HIGGINS. Just so.

LIZA. Like father.

HIGGINS [*grinning, a little taken down*] Without accepting the comparison at all points, Eliza, it's quite true that your father is not a snob, and that he will be quite at home in any station of

PYGMALION

life to which his eccentric destiny may call him. [*Seriously*] The great secret, Eliza, is not having bad manners or good manners or any other particular sort of manners, but having the same manner for all human souls: in short, behaving as if you were in Heaven, where there are no third-class carriages, and one soul is as good as another.

LIZA. Amen. You are a born preacher.

HIGGINS [*irritated*] The question is not whether I treat you rudely, but whether you ever heard me treat anyone else better.

LIZA [*with sudden sincerity*] I dont care how you treat me. I dont mind your swearing at me. I shouldnt mind a black eye: Ive had one before this. But [*standing up and facing him*] I wont be passed over.

HIGGINS. Then get out of my way; for I wont stop for you. You talk about me as if I were a motor bus.

LIZA. So you are a motor bus: all bounce and go, and no consideration for anyone. But I can do without you: dont think I cant.

HIGGINS. I know you can. I told you you could.

LIZA [*wounded, getting away from him to the other side of the ottoman with her face to the hearth*] I know you did, you brute. You wanted to get rid of me.

HIGGINS. Liar.

LIZA. Thank you. [*She sits down with dignity*].

HIGGINS. You never asked yourself, I suppose, whether *I* could do without you.

LIZA [*earnestly*] Dont you try to get round me. Youll have to do without me.

HIGGINS [*arrogant*] I can do without anybody. I have my own soul: my own spark of divine fire. But [*with sudden humility*] I shall miss you, Eliza. [*He sits down near her on the ottoman*]. I have learnt something from your idiotic notions: I confess that humbly and gratefully. And I have grown accustomed to your voice and appearance. I like them, rather.

LIZA. Well, you have both of them on your gramophone and in your book of photographs. When you feel lonely without me, you can turn the machine on. It's got no feelings to hurt.

HIGGINS. I cant turn your soul on. Leave me those feelings; and you can take away the voice and the face. They are not you.

LIZA. Oh, you are a devil. You can twist the heart in a girl as easy as some could twist her arms to hurt her. Mrs Pearce warned me. Time and again she has wanted to leave you; and you always got round her at the last minute. And you dont care a bit for her. And you dont care a bit for me.

HIGGINS. I care for life, for humanity; and you are a part of it that has come my way and been built into my house. What more can you or anyone ask?

LIZA. I wont care for anybody that doesnt care for me.

HIGGINS. Commercial principles, Eliza. Like [reproducing her Covent Garden pronunciation with professional exactness] s'yollin voylets [selling violets], isnt it?

LIZA. Dont sneer at me. It's mean to sneer at me.

HIGGINS. I have never sneered in my life. Sneering doesnt become either the human face or the human soul. I am expressing my righteous contempt for Commercialism. I dont and wont trade in affection. You call me a brute because you couldnt buy a claim on me by fetching my slippers and finding my spectacles. You were a fool: I think a woman fetching a man's slippers is a disgusting sight: did I ever fetch your slippers? I think a good deal more of you for throwing them in my face. No use slaving for me and then saying you want to be cared for: who cares for a slave? If you come back, come back for the sake of good fellowship; for youll get nothing else. Youve had a thousand times as much out of me as I have out of you; and if you dare to set up your little dog's tricks of fetching and carrying slippers against my creation of a Duchess Eliza, I'll slam the door in your silly face.

LIZA. What did you do it for if you didnt care for me?

HIGGINS [*heartily*] Why, because it was my job.

LIZA. You never thought of the trouble it would make for me.

HIGGINS. Would the world ever have been made if its maker had been afraid of making trouble? Making life means making trouble. Theres only one way of escaping trouble; and thats killing things. Cowards, you notice, are always shrieking to have troublesome people killed.

LIZA. I'm no preacher: I dont notice things like that. I notice that you dont notice me.

HIGGINS [*jumping up and walking about intolerantly*] Eliza: youre an idiot. I waste the treasures of my Miltonic mind by spreading them before you. Once for all, understand that I go my way and do my work without caring twopence what happens to either of us. I am not intimidated, like your father and your stepmother. So you can come back or go to the devil: which you please.

LIZA. What am I to come back for?

HIGGINS [*bouncing up on his knees on the ottoman and leaning over it to her*] For the fun of it. Thats why I took you on.

LIZA [*with averted face*] And you may throw me out tomorrow if I dont do everything you want me to?

HIGGINS. Yes; and you may walk out tomorrow if I dont do everything you want me to.

LIZA. And live with my stepmother?

HIGGINS. Yes, or sell flowers.

LIZA. Oh! if I only could go back to my flower basket! I should be independent of both you and father and all the world! Why did you take my independence from me? Why did I give it up? I'm a slave now, for all my fine clothes.

HIGGINS. Not a bit. I'll adopt you as my daughter and settle money on you if you like. Or would you rather marry Pickering?

LIZA [*looking fiercely round at him*] I wouldnt marry you if you asked me; and youre nearer my age than what he is.

PYGMALION

HIGGINS [*gently*] Than he is: not "than what he is."

LIZA [*losing her temper and rising*] I'll talk as I like. Youre not my teacher now.

HIGGINS [*reflectively*] I dont suppose Pickering would, though. He's as confirmed an old bachelor as I am.

LIZA. Thats not what I want; and dont you think it. Ive always had chaps enough wanting me that way. Freddy Hill writes to me twice and three times a day, sheets and sheets.

HIGGINS [*disagreeably surprised*] Damn his impudence! [*He recoils and finds himself sitting on his heels*].

LIZA. He has a right to if he likes, poor lad. And he does love me.

HIGGINS [*getting off the ottoman*] You have no right to encourage him.

LIZA. Every girl has a right to be loved.

HIGGINS. What! By fools like that?

LIZA. Freddy's not a fool. And if he's weak and poor and wants me, may be he'd make me happier than my betters that bully me and dont want me.

HIGGINS. Can he make anything of you? Thats the point.

LIZA. Perhaps I could make something of him. But I never thought of us making anything of one another; and you never think of anything else. I only want to be natural.

HIGGINS. In short, you want me to be as infatuated about you as Freddy? Is that it?

LIZA. No I dont. Thats not the sort of feeling I want from you. And dont you be too sure of yourself or of me. I could have been a bad girl if I'd liked. Ive seen more of some things than you, for all your learning. Girls like me can drag gentlemen down to make love to them easy enough. And they wish each other dead the next minute.

HIGGINS. Of course they do. Then what in thunder are we quarrelling about?

LIZA [*much troubled*] I want a little kindness. I know I'm a

PYGMALION

common ignorant girl, and you a book-learned gentleman; but I'm not dirt under your feet. What I done [*correcting herself*] what I did was not for the dresses and the taxis: I did it because we were pleasant together and I come—came—to care for you; not to want you to make love to me, and not forgetting the difference between us, but more friendly like.

HIGGINS. Well, of course. Thats just how I feel. And how Pickering feels. Eliza: youre a fool.

LIZA. Thats not a proper answer to give me [*she sinks on the chair at the writing-table in tears*].

HIGGINS. It's all youll get until you stop being a common idiot. If youre going to be a lady, youll have to give up feeling neglected if the men you know dont spend half their time snivelling over you and the other half giving you black eyes. If you cant stand the coldness of my sort of life, and the strain of it, go back to the gutter. Work til youre more a brute than a human being; and then cuddle and squabble and drink til you fall asleep. Oh, it's a fine life, the life of the gutter. It's real: it's warm: it's violent: you can feel it through the thickest skin: you can taste it and smell it without any training or any work. Not like Science and Literature and Classical Music and Philosophy and Art. You find me cold, unfeeling, selfish, dont you? Very well: be off with you to the sort of people you like. Marry some sentimental hog or other with lots of money, and a thick pair of lips to kiss you with and a thick pair of boots to kick you with. If you cant appreciate what youve got, youd better get what you can appreciate.

LIZA [*desperate*] Oh, you a r e a cruel tyrant. I cant talk to you: you turn everything against me: I'm always in the wrong. But you know very well all the time that youre nothing but a bully. You know I cant go back to the gutter, as you call it, and that I have no real friends in the world but you and the Colonel. You know well I couldnt bear to live with a low common man after you two; and it's wicked and cruel of you to insult me by pretending I could. You think I must go back to Wimpole Street because I have nowhere else to go but father's. But dont you be too sure that you have me under your feet to be trampled on and talked down. I'll marry Freddy, I will, as soon as I'm able to support him.

HIGGINS [*thunderstruck*] Freddy!!! that young fool! That poor devil who couldnt get a job as an errand boy even if he had the guts to try for it! Woman: do you not understand that I have made you a consort for a king?

LIZA. Freddy loves me: that makes him king enough for me. I dont want him to work: he wasnt brought up to it as I was. I'll go and be a teacher.

HIGGINS. Whatll you teach, in heaven's name?

LIZA. What you taught me. I'll teach phonetics.

HIGGINS. Ha! ha! ha!

LIZA. I'll offer myself as an assistant to that hairyfaced Hungarian.

HIGGINS [*rising in a fury*] What! That impostor! that humbug! that toadying ignoramus! Teach him my methods! my discoveries! You take one step in his direction and I'll wring your neck. [*He lays hands on her*]. Do you hear?

LIZA [*defiantly non-resistant*] Wring away. What do I care? I knew youd strike me some day. [*He lets her go, stamping with rage at having forgotten himself, and recoils so hastily that he stumbles back into his seat on the ottoman*]. Aha! Now I know how to deal with you. What a fool I was not to think of it before! You cant take away the knowledge you gave me. You said I had a finer ear than you. And I can be civil and kind to people, which is more than you can. Aha! [*Purposely dropping her aitches to annoy him*] Thats done you, Enry Iggins, it az. Now I dont care that [*snapping her fingers*] for your bullying and your big talk. I'll advertize it in the papers that your duchess is only a flower girl that you taught, and that she'll teach anybody to be a duchess just the same in six months for a thousand guineas. Oh, when I think of myself crawling under your feet and being trampled on and called names, when all the time I had only to lift up my finger to be as good as you, I could just kick myself.

HIGGINS [*wondering at her*] You damned impudent slut, you! But it's better than snivelling; better than fetching slippers and finding spectacles, isnt it? [*Rising*] By George, Eliza, I said I'd make a woman of you; and I have. I like you like this.

LIZA. Yes: you turn round and make up to me now that I'm not afraid of you, and can do without you.

HIGGINS. Of course I do, you little fool. Five minutes ago you were like a millstone round my neck. Now youre a tower of strength: a consort battleship. You and I and Pickering will be three old bachelors together instead of only two men and a silly girl.

Mrs Higgins returns, dressed for the wedding. Eliza instantly becomes cool and elegant.

MRS HIGGINS. The carriage is waiting, Eliza. Are you ready?

LIZA. Quite. Is the Professor coming?

MRS HIGGINS. Certainly not. He cant behave himself in church. He makes remarks out loud all the time on the clergyman's pronunciation.

LIZA. Then I shall not see you again, Professor. Goodbye. [*She goes to the door*].

MRS HIGGINS [*coming to Higgins*] Goodbye, dear.

HIGGINS. Goodbye, mother. [*He is about to kiss her, when he recollects something*]. Oh, by the way, Eliza, order a ham and a Stilton cheese, will you? And buy me a pair of reindeer gloves, number eights, and a tie to match that new suit of mine. You can choose the color. [*His cheerful, careless, vigorous voice shews that he is incorrigible*].

LIZA [*disdainfully*] Number eights are too small for you if you want them lined with lamb's wool. You have three new ties that you have forgotten in the drawer of your washstand. Colonel Pickering prefers double Gloucester to Stilton; and you dont notice the difference. I telephoned Mrs Pearce this morning not to forget the ham. What you are to do without me I cannot imagine. [*She sweeps out*].

MRS HIGGINS. I'm afraid youve spoilt that girl, Henry. I should be uneasy about you and her if she were less fond of Colonel Pickering.

HIGGINS. Pickering! Nonsense: she's going to marry Freddy. Ha ha! Freddy! Freddy!! Ha ha ha ha ha!!!!! [*He roars with laughter as the play ends*].

* * * * * *

The rest of the story need not be shewn in action, and indeed, would hardly need telling if our imaginations were not so enfeebled by their lazy dependence on the ready-mades and reach-me-downs of the ragshop in which Romance keeps its stock of "happy endings" to misfit all stories. Now, the history of Eliza Doolittle, though called a romance because the transfiguration it records seems exceedingly improbable, is common enough. Such transfigurations have been achieved by hundreds of resolutely ambitious young women since Nell Gwynne set them the example by playing queens and fascinating kings in the theatre in which she began by selling oranges. Nevertheless, people in all directions have assumed, for no other reason than that she became the heroine of a romance, that she must have married the hero of it. This is unbearable, not only because her little drama, if acted on such a thoughtless assumption, must be spoiled, but because the true sequel is patent to anyone with a sense of human nature in general, and of feminine instinct in particular.

Eliza, in telling Higgins she would not marry him if he asked her, was not coquetting: she was announcing a well-considered decision. When a bachelor interests, and dominates, and teaches, and becomes important to a spinster, as Higgins with Eliza, she always, if she has character enough to be capable of it, considers very seriously indeed whether she will play for becoming that bachelor's wife, especially if he is so little interested in marriage that a determined and devoted woman might capture him if she set herself resolutely to do it. Her decision will depend a good deal on whether she is really free to choose; and that, again, will depend on her age and income. If she is at the end of her youth, and has no security for her livelihood, she will marry him because she must marry anybody who will provide for her. But at Eliza's age a good-looking girl does not feel that pressure: she feels free to pick and choose. She is therefore guided by her instinct in the matter. Eliza's instinct tells her not to marry Higgins. It does not tell her to give him up. It is not in the slightest doubt as to his remaining one of the strongest personal interests in her life. It would be very sorely strained if there was another woman likely to supplant her with him. But as she feels sure of him on that last point, she has no doubt at all as to her course, and would not have any, even if the difference of twenty years in age, which seems so great to youth, did not exist between them.

As our own instincts are not appealed to by her conclusion, let us see whether we cannot discover some reason in it. When Higgins excused his indifference to young women on the ground that they had an irresistible rival in his mother, he gave the clue to his inveterate old-bachelordom. The case is uncommon only to the extent that remarkable mothers are uncommon. If an imaginative boy has a sufficiently rich mother who has intelligence, personal grace, dignity of character without harshness, and a cultivated sense of the best art of her time to enable her to make her house beautiful, she sets a standard for him against which very few women can struggle, besides effecting for him a disengagement of his affections, his sense of beauty, and his idealism from his specifically sexual impulses. This makes him a standing puzzle to the huge number of uncultivated people who have been brought up in tasteless homes by commonplace or disagreeable parents, and to whom, consequently, literature, painting, sculpture, music, and affectionate personal relations come as modes of sex if they come at all. The word passion means nothing else to them; and that Higgins could have a passion for phonetics and idealize his mother instead of Eliza, would seem to them absurd and un-natural. Nevertheless, when we look round and see that hardly anyone is too ugly or disagreeable to find a wife or a husband if he or she wants one, whilst many old maids and bachelors are above the average in quality and culture, we cannot help suspecting that the disentanglement of sex from the associations with which it is so commonly confused, a disentanglement which persons of genius achieve by sheer intellectual analysis, is sometimes produced or aided by parental fascination.

Now, though Eliza was incapable of thus explaining to herself Higgins's formidable powers of resistance to the charm that prostrated Freddy at the first glance, she was instinctively aware that she could never obtain a complete grip of him, or come between him and his mother (the first necessity of the married woman). To put it shortly, she knew that for some mysterious reason he had not the makings of a married man in him, according to her conception of a husband as one to whom she would be his nearest and fondest and warmest interest. Even had there been no mother-rival, she would still have refused to accept an interest in herself that was secondary to philosophic interests. Had Mrs Higgins died, there would still have been Milton and the Universal Alphabet. Landor's remark that to those who have the greatest power of loving, love is a secondary affair, would not have recommended Landor to Eliza. Put that along with her resentment of Higgins's domineering superiority, and her mistrust of his coaxing cleverness in getting round her and evading her wrath when he had gone too far with his impetuous bullying, and you will see that Eliza's instinct had good grounds for warning her not to marry her Pygmalion.

And now, whom did Eliza marry? For if Higgins was a predestinate old bachelor, she was most certainly not a predestinate old maid. Well, that can be told very shortly to those who have not guessed it from the indications she has herself given them.

Almost immediately after Eliza is stung into proclaiming her considered determination not to marry Higgins, she mentions the fact that young Mr Frederick Eynsford Hill is pouring out his love for her daily through the post. Now Freddy is young, practically twenty years younger than Higgins: he is a gentleman (or, as Eliza would qualify him, a toff), and speaks like one. He is nicely dressed, is treated by the Colonel as an equal, loves her unaffectedly, and is not her master, nor ever likely to dominate her in spite of his advantage of social standing. Eliza has no use for the foolish romantic tradition that all women love to be mastered, if not actually bullied and beaten. "When you go to women" says Nietzsche "take your whip with you." Sensible despots have never confined that precaution to women: they have taken their whips with them when they have dealt with men, and been slavishly idealized by the men over whom they have flourished the whip much more than by women. No doubt there are slavish women as well as slavish men; and women, like men, admire those that are stronger than themselves. But to admire a strong person and to live under that strong person's thumb are two different things. The weak may not be admired and hero-worshipped; but they are by no means disliked or shunned; and they never seem to have the least difficulty in marrying people who are too good for them. They may fail in emergencies; but life is not one long emergency: it is mostly a string of situations for which no exceptional strength is needed, and with which even rather weak people can cope if they have a stronger partner to help them out. Accordingly, it is a truth everywhere in evidence that strong people, masculine or feminine, not only do not marry stronger people, but do not shew any preference for them in selecting their friends. When a lion meets another with a louder roar "the first lion thinks the last a bore." The man or woman who feels strong enough for two, seeks for every other quality in a partner than strength.

The converse is also true. Weak people want to marry strong people who do not frighten them too much; and this often leads them to make the mistake we describe metaphorically as "biting off more than they can chew." They want too much for too little; and when the bargain is unreasonable beyond all bearing, the union becomes impossible: it ends in the weaker party being either discarded or borne as a cross, which is worse. People who are not only weak, but silly or obtuse as well, are often in these difficulties.

This being the state of human affairs, what is Eliza fairly sure to do when she is placed between Freddy and Higgins? Will she look forward to a lifetime of fetching Higgins's slippers or to a lifetime of Freddy fetching hers? There can be no doubt about the answer. Unless Freddy is biologically repulsive to her, and Higgins biologically attractive to a degree that overwhelms all her other instincts, she will, if she marries either of them, marry Freddy.

And that is just what Eliza did.

Complications ensued; but they were economic, not romantic. Freddy had no money and no occupation. His mother's jointure, a last relic of the opulence of Largelady Park, had enabled her to struggle along in Earlscourt with an air of gentility, but not to procure any serious secondary education for her children, much less give the boy a profession. A clerkship at thirty shillings a week was beneath Freddy's dignity, and extremely distasteful to him besides. His prospects consisted of a hope that if he kept up appearances somebody would do something for him. The something appeared vaguely to his imagination as a private secretary-ship or a sinecure of some sort. To his mother it perhaps appeared as a marriage to some lady of means who could not resist her boy's niceness. Fancy her feelings when he married a flower girl who had become disclassed under extraordinary circumstances which were now notorious!

It is true that Eliza's situation did not seem wholly ineligible. Her father, though formerly a dustman, and now fantastically disclassed, had become extremely popular in the smartest society by a social talent which triumphed over every prejudice and every disadvantage. Rejected by the middle class, which he loathed, he had shot up at once into the highest circles by his wit, his dustmanship (which he carried like a banner), and his Nietzschean transcendence of good and evil. At intimate ducal dinners he sat on the right hand of the Duchess; and in country houses he smoked in the pantry and was made much of by the butler when he was not feeding in the dining room and being consulted by cabinet ministers. But he found it almost as hard to do all this on four thousand a year as Mrs Eynsford Hill to live in Earlscourt on an income so pitiably smaller that I have not the heart to disclose its exact figure. He absolutely refused to add the last straw to his burden by contributing to Eliza's support.

Thus Freddy and Eliza, now Mr and Mrs Eynsford Hill, would have spent a penniless honeymoon but for a wedding present of £500 from the Colonel to Eliza. It lasted a long time because Freddy did not know how to spend money, never having had any to spend, and Eliza, socially trained by a pair of old bachelors, wore her clothes as long as they held together and looked pretty, without the least regard to their being many months out of fashion. Still, £500 will not last two young people for ever; and they both knew, and Eliza felt as well, that they must shift for themselves in the end. She could quarter herself on Wimpole Street because it had come to be her home; but she was quite aware that she ought not to quarter Freddy there, and that it would not be good for his character if she did.

Not that the Wimpole Street bachelors objected. When she consulted them, Higgins declined to be bothered about her housing problem when that solution was so simple. Eliza's desire to have Freddy in the house with her seemed of no more importance than if she had wanted an extra piece of bedroom furniture. Pleas as to Freddy's character, and the moral obligation on him to earn his own living, were lost on Higgins. He denied that Freddy had any character, and declared that if he tried to do any useful work some competent person would have the trouble of undoing it: a procedure involving a net loss to the community, and great unhappiness to Freddy himself, who was obviously intended by Nature for such light work as amusing Eliza, which, Higgins declared, was a much more useful and honorable occupation than working in the city. When Eliza referred again to her project of teaching phonetics, Higgins abated not a jot of his violent opposition to it. He said she was not within ten years of being qualified to meddle with his pet subject; and as it was evident that the Colonel agreed with him, she felt she could not go against them in this grave matter, and that she had no right, without Higgins's consent, to exploit the knowledge he had given her; for his knowledge seemed to her as much his private property as his watch: Eliza was no communist. Besides, she was superstitiously devoted to them both, more entirely and frankly after her marriage than before it.

It was the Colonel who finally solved the problem, which had cost him much perplexed cogitation. He one day asked Eliza, rather shyly, whether she had quite given up her notion of keeping a flower shop. She replied that she had thought of it, but had put it out of her head, because the Colonel had said, that day at Mrs Higgins's, that it would never do. The Colonel confessed that when he said that, he had not quite recovered from the dazzling impression of the day before. They broke the matter to Higgins that evening. The sole comment vouchsafed by him very nearly led to a serious quarrel with Eliza. It was to the effect that she would have in Freddy an ideal errand boy.

Freddy himself was next sounded on the subject. He said he had been thinking of a shop himself; though it had presented itself to his pennilessness as a small place in which Eliza should sell tobacco at one counter whilst he sold newspapers at the opposite one. But he agreed that it would be extraordinarily jolly to go early every morning with Eliza to Covent Garden and buy flowers on the scene of their first meeting: a sentiment which earned him many kisses from his wife. He added that he had always been afraid to propose anything of the sort, because Clara would make an awful row about a step that must damage her matrimonial chances, and his mother could not be expected to like it after clinging for so many years to that step of the social ladder on which retail trade is impossible.

This difficulty was removed by an event highly unexpected by Freddy's mother. Clara, in the course of her incursions into those artistic circles which were the highest within her reach, discovered that her conversational qualifications were expected to include a grounding in the novels of Mr H. G. Wells. She borrowed them in various directions so energetically that she swallowed them all within two months. The result was a conversion of a kind quite common today. A modern Acts of the Apostles would fill fifty whole Bibles if anyone were capable of writing it.

Poor Clara, who appeared to Higgins and his mother as a disagreeable and ridiculous person, and to her own mother as in some inexplicable way a social failure, had never seen herself in either light; for, though to some extent ridiculed and mimicked in West Kensington like everybody else there, she was accepted as a rational and normal—or shall we say inevitable?—sort of human being. At worst they called her The Pusher; but to them no more than to herself had it ever occurred that she was pushing the air, and pushing it in a wrong direction. Still, she was not happy. She was growing desperate. Her one asset, the fact that her mother was what the Epsom greengrocer called a carriage lady, had no exchange value, apparently. It had prevented her from getting educated, because the only education she could have afforded was education with the Earlscourt greengrocer's daughter. It had led her to seek the society of her mother's class; and that class simply would not have her, because she was much poorer than the greengrocer, and, far from being able to afford a maid, could not afford even a housemaid, and had to scrape along at home with an illiberally treated general servant. Under such circumstances nothing could give her an air of being a genuine product of Largelady Park. And yet its tradition made her regard a marriage with anyone within her reach as an unbearable humiliation. Commercial people and professional people in a small way were odious to her. She ran after painters and novelists; but she did not charm them; and her bold attempts to pick up and practise artistic and literary talk irritated them. She was, in short, an utter failure, an ignorant, incompetent, pretentious, unwelcome, penniless, useless little snob; and though she did not admit these disqualifications (for nobody ever faces unpleasant truths of this kind until the possibility of a way out dawns on them) she felt their effects too keenly to be satisfied with her position.

Clara had a startling eyeopener when, on being suddenly wakened to enthusiasm by a girl of her own age who dazzled her and produced in her a gushing desire to take her for a model and gain her friendship, she discovered that this exquisite apparition had graduated from the gutter in a few months time. It shook her so violently, that when Mr H. G. Wells lifted her on the point of his puissant pen, and placed her at the angle of view from which the life she was leading and the society to which she clung appeared in its true relation to real human needs and worthy social structure, he effected a conversion and a conviction of sin comparable to the most sensational feats of General Booth or Gypsy Smith. Clara's snobbery went bang. Life suddenly began to move with her. Without knowing how or why, she began to make friends and enemies. Some of the acquaintances to whom she had been a tedious or indifferent or ridiculous affliction, dropped her: others became cordial. To her amazement she found that some "quite nice" people were saturated with Wells, and that this accessibility to ideas was the secret of their niceness. People she had thought deeply religious, and had tried to conciliate on that tack with disastrous results, suddenly took an interest in her, and revealed a hostility to conventional religion which she had never conceived possible except among the most desperate characters. They made her read Galsworthy; and Galsworthy exposed the vanity of Largelady Park and finished her. It exasperated her to think that the dungeon in which she had languished for so many unhappy years had been unlocked all the time, and that the impulses she had so carefully struggled with and stifled for the sake of keeping well with society, were precisely those by which alone she could have come into any sort of sincere human contact. In the radiance of these discoveries, and the tumult of their reaction, she made a fool of herself as freely and conspicuously as when she so rashly adopted Eliza's expletive in Mrs Higgins's drawing room; for the new-born Wellsian had to find her bearings almost as ridiculously as a baby; but nobody hates a baby for its ineptitudes, or thinks the worse of it for trying to eat the matches; and Clara lost no friends by her follies. They laughed at her to her face this time; and she had to defend herself and fight it out as best she could.

When Freddy paid a visit to Earlscourt (which he never did when he could possibly help it) to make the desolating announcement that he and his Eliza were thinking of blackening the Largelady scutcheon by opening a shop, he found the little household already convulsed by a prior announcement from Clara that she also was going to work in an old furniture shop in Dover Street, which had been started by a fellow Wellsian. This appointment Clara owed, after all, to her old social accomplishment of Push. She had made up her mind that, cost what it might, she would see Mr Wells in the flesh; and she had achieved her end at a garden party. She had better luck than so rash an enterprise deserved. Mr Wells came up to her expectations. Age had not withered him, nor could custom stale his infinite variety in half an hour. His pleasant neatness and compactness, his small hands and feet, his teeming ready brain, his unaffected accessibility, and a certain fine apprehensiveness which stamped him as susceptible from his topmost hair to his tipmost toe, proved irresistible. Clara talked of nothing else for weeks and weeks afterwards.

114

And as she happened to talk to the lady of the furniture shop, and that lady also desired above all things to know Mr Wells and sell pretty things to him, she offered Clara a job on the chance of achieving that end through her.

And so it came about that Eliza's luck held, and the expected opposition to the flower shop melted away. The shop is in the arcade of a railway station not very far from the Victoria and Albert Museum; and if you live in that neighborhood you may go there any day and buy a buttonhole from Eliza.

Now here is a last opportunity for romance. Would you not like to be assured that the shop was an immense success, thanks to Eliza's charms and her early business experience in Covent Garden? Alas! the truth is the truth: the shop did not pay for a long time, simply because Eliza and her Freddy did not know how to keep it. True, Eliza had not to begin at the very beginning: she knew the names and prices of the cheaper flowers; and her elation was unbounded when she found that Freddy, like all youths educated at cheap, pretentious, and thoroughly inefficient schools, knew a little Latin. It was very little, but enough to make him appear to her a Porson or Bentley, and to put him at his ease with botanical nomenclature. Unfortunately he knew nothing else; and Eliza, though she could count money up to eighteen shillings or so, and had acquired a certain familiarity with the language of Milton from her struggles to qualify herself for winning Higgins's bet, could not write out a bill without utterly disgracing the establishment. Freddy's power of stating in Latin that Balbus built a wall and that Gaul was divided into three parts did not carry with it the slightest knowledge of accounts or business: Colonel Pickering had to explain to him what a cheque book and a bank account meant. And the pair were by no means easily teachable. Freddy backed up Eliza in her obstinate refusal to believe that they could save money by engaging a bookkeeper with some knowledge of the business. How, they argued, could you possibly save money by going to extra expense when you already could not make both ends meet? But the Colonel, after making the ends meet over and over again, at last gently insisted; and Eliza, humbled to the dust by having to beg from him so often, and stung by the uproarious derision of Higgins, to whom the notion of Freddy succeeding at anything was a joke that never palled, grasped the fact that business, like phonetics, has to be learned.

On the piteous spectacle of the pair spending their evenings in shorthand schools and polytechnic classes, learning bookkeeping and typewriting with incipient junior clerks, male and female, from the elementary schools, let me not dwell. There were even classes at the London School of Economics, and a humble personal appeal to the director of that institution to recommend a course bearing on the flower business. He, being a humorist, explained to them the method of the celebrated Dickensian essay on Chinese Metaphysics by the gentleman who read an article on China and an article on Metaphysics and combined the information. He suggested that they should combine the London School with Kew Gardens. Eliza, to whom the procedure of the Dickensian gentleman seemed perfectly correct (as in fact it was) and not in the least funny (which was only her ignorance), took the advice with entire gravity. But the effort that cost her the deepest humiliation was a request to Higgins, whose pet artistic fancy, next to Milton's verse, was caligraphy, and who himself wrote a most beautiful Italian hand, that he would teach her to write. He declared that she was congenitally incapable of forming a single letter worthy of the least of Milton's words; but she persisted; and again he suddenly threw himself into the task of teaching her with a combination of stormy intensity, concentrated patience, and occasional bursts of interesting disquisition on the beauty and nobility, the august mission and destiny, of human handwriting. Eliza ended by acquiring an extremely uncommercial script which was a positive extension of her personal beauty, and spending three times as much on stationery as anyone else

116

because certain qualities and shapes of paper became indispensable to her. She could not even address an envelope in the usual way because it made the margins all wrong.

Their commercial schooldays were a period of disgrace and despair for the young couple. They seemed to be learning nothing about flower shops. At last they gave it up as hopeless, and shook the dust of the shorthand schools, and the polytechnics, and the London School of Economics from their feet for ever. Besides, the business was in some mysterious way beginning to take care of itself. They had somehow forgotten their objections to employing other people. They came to the conclusion that their own way was the best, and that they had really a remarkable talent for business. The Colonel, who had been compelled for some years to keep a sufficient sum on current account at his bankers to make up their deficits, found that the provision was unnecessary: the young people were prospering. It is true that there was not quite fair play between them and their competitors in trade. Their week-ends in the country cost them nothing, and saved them the price of their Sunday dinners; for the motor car was the Colonel's; and he and Higgins paid the hotel bills. Mr F. Hill, florist and greengrocer (they soon discovered that there was money in asparagus; and asparagus led to other vegetables), had an air which stamped the business as classy; and in private life he was still Frederick Eynsford Hill, Esquire. Not that there was any swank about him: nobody but Eliza knew that he had been christened Frederick Challoner. Eliza herself swanked like anything.

That is all. That is how it has turned out. It is astonishing how much Eliza still manages to meddle in the housekeeping at Wimpole Street in spite of the shop and her own family. And it is notable that though she never nags her husband, and frankly loves the Colonel as if she were his favorite daughter, she has never got out of the habit of nagging Higgins that was established on the fatal night when she won his bet for him. She snaps his head off on the faintest provocation, or on none. He no longer dares to tease her by assuming an abysmal inferiority of Freddy's mind to his own. He storms and bullies and derides; but she stands up to him so ruthlessly that the Colonel has to ask her from time to time to be kinder to Higgins; and it is the only request of his that brings a mulish expression into her face. Nothing but some emergency or calamity great enough to break down all likes and dislikes, and throw them both back on their common humanity—and may they be spared any such trial!— will ever alter this. She knows that Higgins does not need her, just as her father did not need her. The very scrupulousness with which he told her that day that he had become used to having her there, and dependent on her for all sorts of little services, and that he should miss her if she went away (it would never have occurred to Freddy or the Colonel to say anything of the sort) deepens her inner certainty that she is "no more to him than them slippers"; yet she has a sense, too, that his indifference is deeper than the infatuation of commoner souls. She is immensely interested in him. She has even secret mischievous moments in which she wishes she could get him alone, on a desert island, away from all ties and with nobody else in the world to consider, and just drag him off his pedestal and see him making love like any common man. We all have private imaginations of that sort. But when it comes to business, to the life that she really leads as distinguished from the life of dreams and fancies, she likes Freddy and she likes the Colonel; and she does not like Higgins and Mr Doolittle. Galatea never does quite like Pygmalion: his relation to her is too godlike to be altogether agreeable.

Glossary: reading the text

Preface

1 *sequel*   see pages 105-18 for Shaw's long sequel to the play.

accessible   within reach, available.

phonetic   concerning the sounds of spoken language.

Alexander Melville Bell   (1819-1905) son of Alexander Graham Bell; worked a lot with deaf mutes.

Visible Speech   invention of Melville Bell: a type of alphabet using graphic diagrams to represent speech.

Alexander J Ellis   English writer on phonetics who wanted to reform English spelling.

Henry Sweet (1845-1912) British phonetician and philologist (one who studies the science and background of language). Published many books on language and grammar, devised two types of phonetic alphabet based on the work of Bell and Ellis. Shaw points out later in this preface that Higgins is not a portrait of Sweet but there are touches of Sweet in *Pygmalion.*

conciliatory   bringing opposites together to agree to things.

Ibsen   (1828-1906) Norwegian playwright who introduced many modern elements into late nineteenth and early twentieth-century drama.

Samuel Butler (1835-1902) English satirist who spoke out against hypocrisy in modern morals.

Satanic contempt   devil-like scorn.

2 *Joseph Chamberlain*   (1836-1914) British statesman; colonial secretary in the Government who worked hard to promote imperial expansion.

derisive   mocking, scornful.

libellous   falsely damaging a person's reputation in writing.

repudiation   denial, refusal to recognise.

2 *Readership*   University post with specific responsibilities for research.

Current Shorthand   Sweet's system of lines and strokes to represent phonetics.

four and sixpenny manual   this would have been written as 4/6d, the equivalent of $22\frac{1}{2}$ new pence. See 'A note on money', page xix.

3 *Pitman*   (1813-1897) the inventor of Shorthand – thirty-eight symbols to represent sounds of vowels and consonants.

Sybil   Sibyls were women in Greek mythology who foretold the future. The most famous one wrote her prophecies on leaves so people had to be careful to read them before the wind blew them away.

Gregg shorthand   in 1888 John Robert Gregg published a different kind of shorthand.

4 *Russian size alphabet*   this Cyrillic alphabet has thirty-two letters (the English alphabet has twenty-six); originally it had even more.

Robert Bridges   (1844-1930) famous English poet who was also interested in spelling and phonetics.

5 *didactic*   intended to instruct.

wiseacre   silly person who thinks she or he is clever.

Ruy Blas   verse drama written in 1838 by the French writer Victor Hugo.

Act 1

7 *Cab*   short for taxi cab.

St Paul's church   designed by Inigo Jones (1573-1651) in the centre of Covent Garden; known as The Actors' Church, it is still used for memorial services for people of the theatre.

Covent Garden   see 'London theatres', pages xviii-xix.

He wont get no cab not until   in Standard English this would be: He won't get a cab until…

half-past eleven   most theatres closed at 11pm. Many people needed cabs to take them home.

7 *gumption*   sense, courage.

Southampton Street   in the Covent Garden area.

evening dress   people would dress up to go to the theatre – it was a formal occasion for those sitting in the best seats. Men wore white tie and tails; women wore long dresses.

8 *Charing Cross; Ludgate Circus*   famous landmarks at the west and east ends of The Strand, which runs along the Covent Garden area to the south.

Hammersmith   in west London.

Strandwards   towards The Strand; see note above.

flower girl   girls like Eliza sold bunches of flowers to passers-by.

Nah then, Freddy: look wh'y' gowin, deah   now then Freddy, look where you're going, dear.

Theres menners f'yer! Tǝ-oo banches o voylets trod into the mad   there's manners for you! Two bunches of violets trodden into the mud.

plinth   square block at the base of a column, used as a pedestal.

9 *Ow, eez yǝ-ooa san, is e? Wal, fewd dan y' dǝ-ooty bawmz a mather should, eed now bettern to spawl a pore gel's flahrzn then ran awy athaht pyin. Will yǝ-oo py me f'them?*   oh, he's your son, is he? Well, if you had done your duty by him as a mother should, he would know better than to spoil a poor girl's flowers and then run away without paying. Will you pay me for them?

sixpence   now the equivalent of $2\frac{1}{2}$ pence.

tanner   slang word for sixpence. See also 'A note on money', page xix.

10 *sovereign; half-a-crown; tuppence; hapence*   see 'A note on money', page xix.

11 *hubbub*   confusion, noise.

deprecating   showing disapproval.

hollerin   shouting.

tec   detective (slang).

aw rawt   all right.

11 *bə-oots* boots (policemen's feet were said to be large owing to walking the beat).

copper's nark police informer (the word 'nark' comes from the Romany word 'nak' meaning nose).

12 *Cheer ap, Keptin; n'baw ya flahr orf a pore gel* cheer up, Captain; and buy a flower from a poor girl. (Captain here is just used as a mark of respect.)

agen against.

molestation interference.

Selsey town in Sussex, on the south coast of England.

Lisson Grove west London, near Marylebone, a slum area at the time of the play.

Park Lane street running along one side of Hyde Park in Mayfair, the most fashionable part of London.

13 *Hoxton* at that time slum area in north-east London.

Aint no call to meddle with me, he aint he has no reason to interfere with me, he hasn't.

I dont want to have no truck with him I don't want to have any business with him.

Cheltenham, Harrow, Cambridge, India the implication is that the gentleman had a conventional upper-class upbringing and career: born in Cheltenham, in Gloucestershire; educated at the public school, Harrow; university at Cambridge and the Army in India (then part of the British Empire).

toff slang for gentleman.

14 *pneumownia* pneumonia.

Earlscourt in west London, at the time a middle-class area.

Epsom town in Surrey (south England), home of the famous Derby race.

15 *Anwell* Hanwell – district in the western suburbs of London, where there was at the time an asylum for mentally disturbed people.

worrited and chivied worried and harassed.

GLOSSARY

15 *brogue* accent.

Kentish Town in north-west London, a slum area at that time.

16 *Shakespear* (1564-1616) English playwright, probably the greatest and most famous in the world (usually spelt 'Shakespeare').

Milton (1608-1674) one of England's greatest poets whose most famous work is *Paradise Lost*, written when Milton was blind.

Garn! slang for 'go on'.

17 *Spoken Sanscrit* Sanskrit is an ancient and sacred language of India.

Wimpole Street in the centre of the doctors' area near Harley Street, in the West End of London.

Carlton famous hotel then in the Haymarket, near Piccadilly.

lets have a jaw let's have a chat.

mendacity untruthfulness.

a couple of florins two-shilling pieces; see 'A note on money', page xix.

18 *Angel Court, Drury Lane* just round the corner from Covent Garden.

A shilling see 'A note on money', page xix.

19 *irreducible* incapable of being reduced.

prodigal lavish, wasteful.

miscellaneous consisting of several kinds.

---

1 Look carefully at the actions and words of The Daughter (Clara) and Freddy. What are the differences in the way they both talk to and react towards The Flower Girl (Eliza)? Make a list first to help.

2 Why do you think the bystanders are important in the act?

3 How does The Note Taker (Higgins) behave towards Eliza from the moment Eliza finds out someone has been listening to her (from the bottom of page 10)?

4 What good qualities do you feel Eliza has in this act?

5 From all the characters in this short act, who appears to you to have the best manners? Give examples of their good manners.

5 From all the characters in this short act, who appears to you to have the best manners? Give examples of their good manners.

6 What do you think is going to happen to The Flower Girl in the rest of the play? Which other characters will be important to the main action?

7 Why do you think Shaw wrote a lot of Eliza's speeches phonetically (spelling words so that her dialect comes through to the reader)? Would the opening of the play be better with the words spelt normally?

Act 2

20 *phonograph*   first type of record player, invented in 1863 by Thomas A Eddison.

laryngoscope   apparatus which, by a combination of mirrors, makes it possible to inspect a patient's larynx and throat.

singing flames   apparatus for creating and regulating sounds.

coal-scuttle   container keeping coal to go on an open fire.

Piranesi   (1720-1778) Italian engraver.

mezzotint   method of engraving copper or steel.

21 *frock-coat*   man's long double-breasted jacket – nearly knee length.

petulance   irritation.

22 *Bell's Visible Speech*   see note to page 1.

Romic   one of Sweet's systems for a phonetic alphabet. See note to page 1.

pathos   quality arousing pity.

lingo   manner of speaking (slang).

23 *baggage*   cheeky girl.

Tottenham Court Road   long road in London, now famous for music and sound system shops.

zif   as if.

24 *Youd had a drop in*   you'd been drinking.

25 *eighteenpence*   this would have been written as 18d or 1/6d. Equivalent of $7\frac{1}{2}$ new pence.

25 *have the face*   have the nerve.

shilling   see 'A note on money', page xix.

sixty or seventy guineas   a guinea was an English gold coin worth 21 shillings. Seventy guineas was £73.10s (now the value would be nearer £800).

27 *Monkey Brand*   very strong soap used for cleaning kitchen pots and pans.

Whiteley   famous London store of the day.

prudery   behaviour of someone who snubs anything that is not decent by their standards. (Higgins is suggesting that Eliza's lower-class background has given her the wrong sort of shame.)

zephyr   west wind.

modulation   musical change in the voice.

28 *elocutionary style*   style of pronouncing things in Standard English.

off his chump   out of his mind.

balmies   mad men.

didnt want no   did not want any.

32 *plaints*   complaints.

33 *copper*   container for boiling and washing clothes by hand.

34 *frowzy*   dirty, unpleasant smelling.

37 *certain word*   this would have referred to the swear word *bloody* (see 'Critical reaction', pages xiii-xv).

judicial   concerning the Law.

alliteration   repetition of the same consonant at the beginning of a series of words.

slovenly   untidy.

38 *benzine*   inflammable liquid from petrol, used to remove grease stains.

diffident   modest.

arbitrary   not bound by rules.

blackguard   criminal (term of abuse).

39 *magisterially*   in a masterful way.

Governor   Cockney expression for Sir.

39 *Hounslow*   west London suburb.

40 *fairity*   fair play.

audacity   boldness, nerve.

rhetoric   art of using language and making speeches.

mendacity   see note to page 17.

42 *proximity*   nearness.

43 *rough justice*   without recourse to the Law.

44 *Cabinet*   committee of the most important Government ministers with the Prime Minister at the head.

ginger   spirit, life.

45 *pauperize*   turn into a beggar.

spree   outing, usually involving spending money.

prudent   careful.

46 *deferentially*   respectfully.

48 *collecting dust*   dust here used as slang for money.

navvy   worker on roads or buildings.

cut   ignore.

50 *cep*   except.

---

1   What methods does Higgins use to get Eliza to do what he wants (from page 22 to page 32)?

2   Why does Mrs Pearce think that Higgins's plan will go wrong?

3   Do you think the act would have more or less dramatic effect if Higgins were more polite to Eliza? Give reasons for your point of view.

4   From this act what do you learn of Higgins's views about women?

5   After Doolittle's long speeches why does Higgins end up giving him the money?

6   The entrance of Doolittle is very sudden. What does his appearance add to the discussion on class?

7 How does Mrs Pearce treat:
- Eliza?
- Higgins?

Act 3

51 *Chelsea Embankment* long road overlooking the Thames in an arty area of London.

Morris and Burne Jones William Morris (1834-1896), artist, craftsman, poet and designer of wallpaper, furniture and fabrics; Edward Burne Jones (1833-1898), artist who worked with Morris. Both had a lot of influence on interior decorating and furnishing.

chintz cotton printed in several colours.

ottoman roughly circular type of sofa, without arms or back.

Whistler (1834-1903) American artist who lived in France and England.

Cecil Lawson (1851-1882) landscape painter.

Rubens (1577-1640) Dutch painter.

Rossettian long and flowing dresses as seen in the paintings of Dante Gabriel Rossetti (1828-1882).

estheticism love of beautiful things. Shaw uses the American spelling; English spelling would be '*ae*stheticism'.

Chippendale eighteenth-century furniture designer and maker.

Inigo Jones (1573-1651) architect who designed many fine buildings and worked on the layout for the Covent Garden Piazza.

52 *at-home day* in 'polite society', a time set aside for someone to receive guests into their home.

small talk light conversation, for example, about the weather.

53 *getting on like a house on fire*   getting on very well together.

54 *bravado*   boastful behaviour.

55 *Battersea Park*   large park in south-west London.

Ahdedo?   how do you do? (said in very posh way).

56 *Royal Society's soirees*   social gatherings held by the Royal Society (founded in 1645 to further scientific learning).

57 *pedantic*   trying to be very precise in things.

58 *divan*   couch

fender   fireguard.

barometrical   indicating weather changes.

done the old woman in   killed the old woman.

she come through diptheria   she survived diptheria, an infectious disease.

59 *them as*   those who.

62 *sanguinary*   referring to the word 'bloody'.

63 *bee in bonnet*   obsession.

65 *Beethoven and Brahms*   famous nineteenth-century composers.

Lehar   (1870-1948) Hungarian composer of light operas.

Lionel Monckton   (1862-1924) English composer of musical comedies.

66 *Ripping*   upper-class slang for excellent.

awning   covering to act as shelter from sun and rain.

67 *whiskered Pandour*   moustached eighteenth-century Hungarian soldier.

Maestro   master, teacher.

68 *swells*   slang for rich people.

Clerkenwell   district of London which was a centre for watch and clock-makers.

69 *somnambulist*   sleepwalker.

debutante   name given to a younger woman during her first social season – a time of going to the parties and functions for the upper classes for a few months each year.

70 *Mrs Langtry* Lillie Langtry (1852-1929), famous actress and mistress of King Edward VII.

71 *Magyar* Hungarian.

Morganatic marriage between people of unequal rank (used for a private marriage between a king and a commoner who is not elevated to queen).

---

1 At Mrs Higgins's at-home day Miss Eynsford Hill says, *If people would only be frank and say what they really think!* Why does Eliza's small talk cause both amusement and shock?

2 What qualities does Mrs Higgins have that make her appear to have more common sense and compassion than her son, Henry?

3 When Mrs Higgins says, *No, you two infinitely stupid male creatures: the problem of what is to be done with her afterwards*, she is echoing the thought of a character in Act 2. Who is that character? What are the reactions of Higgins and Pickering to Mrs Higgins's comment?

4 How does Shaw make sure that there is a lot of dramatic tension in the embassy reception scene, even though Eliza says very little throughout?

5 Look carefully at the character of Pickering here and in the previous acts.

   - How does he differ from Higgins?
   - What sort of man do you feel he is?
   - Does he treat Eliza any differently from Higgins and Doolittle?

Act 4

72 *La Fanciulla del Golden West* 'The Girl of the Golden West' – opera by the Italian composer Puccini (1910).

73 *coroneted billet-doux* personal love letter with a printed crest.

tomfoolery foolishness.

74 *purgatory* state of pain, distress.

74 *superlatively*   of the highest degree.

75 *Presumptuous*   forward, taking for granted.

77 *condescending*   offensively being nice; patronising.

Tosh   slang for rubbish.

78 *togs*   slang for clothes.

millennium   height of happiness (a time when all misery in the world will supposedly end).

79 *perfunctorily*   done as routine; carelessly.

decorum   correct behaviour.

81 *To make a hole in it*   to jump into it and commit suicide by drowning.

82 *Wimbledon Common*   open parkland in Wimbledon, south-west suburb in London.

---

1   This act is very short. In the scene between Eliza and Higgins there are many stage directions which help to show the tensions between the characters. Looking at the directions *and* the dialogue explain why Eliza is so upset.

2   In this act Higgins refers to Eliza as a *heartless guttersnipe*; in Act 2 he called her *baggage*. What effect does Higgins's language and name-calling have on Eliza and the reader or audience?

3   Do you think there is any future for Freddy and Eliza following their meeting at the end of the act?

4   What do you predict will happen in the final act?

Act 5

83 *bolted*   run off.

85 *Genteel*   well-bred in manners.

resplendently   brilliantly, shining.

patent leather   made of varnished soft black leather with a permanent shine.

85 *Providence* care of God.

86 *blighter* Cockney term: a scamp.

87 *worrited* worried.

88 *dye my hair* dye his grey hair black – otherwise he might look too old for work.

skilly gruel served to people in the workhouses in the nineteenth century.

Char Bydis Charybidis was a dangerous whirlpool opposite another one called Scylla in the Straits of Messina (between Italy and Sicily) in Greek mythology. Many sailors lost their lives there.

95 *spraddling* sprawling.

St George's, Hanover Square Church used for fashionable weddings in London's West End.

96 *Brougham* early motor car or one-horse carriage.

magnanimous generous.

97 *chaperoned* accompanied for sake of propriety.

98 *to get round me* persuade me by being nice to me.

99 *commercial* business.

103 *ignoramus* ignorant person.

---

1 What do you suppose Higgins told the police when informing them Eliza had *bolted*?

2 *Done to me! Ruined me. Destroyed my happiness*, explains Doolittle to Mrs Higgins on page 86. Why is Doolittle more unhappy now than he appeared to be in his first entrance in Act 2?

3 Why is Doolittle so angry with Higgins?

4 What is different about Eliza in this act compared with previous acts?

5 On page 97 Eliza comments that Higgins seems to treat her like her father. What other similarities can you find between Higgins and Doolittle in this act and others?

6 In the final scene between Eliza and Higgins (pages 97-105), they argue about everything. Who do you think presents the better arguments? Do you think either character ends up the winner?

Epilogue

105 *Nell Gwynne* (1650-1687) orange seller who became an actress in Drury Lane Theatre and mistress to King Charles II.

coquetting flirting.

107 *Landor* Walter Savage (1775-1864), poet and writer.

108 *Nietzsche* (1844-1900) German philosopher whose views were examined a little in Shaw's play *Man and Superman*, in which the playwright looked at the idea of what he called the life force.

109 *obtuse* stupid.

jointure property.

opulence wealth.

sinecure position held without any work to do.

112 *H G Wells* (1866-1946) famous novelist and science fiction writer. Shaw had a long standing disagreement with him over politics and other matters.

West Kensington in west London; Earls Court is in the centre of the district.

113 *on the point of his puissant pen* puissant means powerful. In one of Wells's novels (*Ann Veronica*), he looked at the kind of woman Clara wanted to be.

General Booth William Booth (1829-1912), founder of the Salvation Army.

Gypsy Smith Rodney Smith (1860-1947), travelling preacher whose parents were gypsies.

GLOSSARY

114 *Galsworthy* John (1867-1933), English novelist who wrote *The Forsyte Saga*.

languished lay wasting.

expletive swear word.

scutcheon usually escutcheon; shield bearing the family's coat of arms.

Dover Street between Victoria and Westminster in London.

Age had not withered him, nor could custom stale his infinite variety Shaw is making fun of Wells liking women by changing part of the famous lines from Shakespeare's *Antony and Cleopatra*: *Age cannot wither her, nor custom stale/ Her infinite variety.*

115 *Victoria and Albert Museum* famous museum in South Kensington in London.

Porson; Bentley eighteenth-century scholars.

116 *London School of Economics* college of London University, founded in 1895 by Sidney and Beatrice Webb, friends and political colleagues of Shaw.

Kew Gardens in west London; home of the famous botanical gardens with collections of plants and flowers from all over the world.

caligraphy beautiful handwriting (usually spelt 'calligraphy').

Study programme

General impressions

1. Look at the words and phrases listed below. Take ten (in any order) and write two or three sentences to say why that word or phrase might have a lot to do with *Pygmalion*:

clothes	poverty
snobbery	love
money	funny accents
the class system	London
behaviour	wealth
a private bet	long words
control	impressions
morals	society
parents and children	standards
small, local communities	friendship
families	use of language

2. Now decide on no more than five of these words which you think best sum up the main themes of *Pygmalion*. You need to think about the main ideas which run throughout the play.

When you have decided, write a paragraph for each word explaining why you think it describes a main theme in the play. Each paragraph should contain a minimum of four sentences, but you could write a lot more if you think about the whole play.

Characters

The main characters

1. Look at the words, phrases or sentences on pages 136-7 from each act. Write down:

- which character is speaking;
- why they say what is quoted;
- what part of the play the words come from;
- what their words tell you about the characters.

A chart may help.

Quote	Character	Reason	Part of play	What it reveals
Sixpence thrown away! Really...	Clara	Doesn't want her mother to spend more than the flowers are worth.	Act 1 in the rain.	Clara is behaving like a snob. She has in mind a better use for the money. She has no thought to spare for those poorer than herself.
I'm a respectable girl: so help me...	Eliza	She wants to show that she's honest and has not done anything wrong.	Act 1 after the note taker is seen to be writing down her words.	Eliza is doing an honest job and she does not want people to think she is not respectable.
I find that the moment I let myself make friends with a woman, I become selfish and tyrannical.	Higgins	He and Pickering are discussing the character of men once they become involved with women.	Act 2 whilst Eliza is having a bath.	Higgins would much prefer to get on with his life alone. He thinks women upset and ruin everything.

135

Now continue the chart using the following quotations, which are in chronological act order:

Act 2

- *I hope it's understood that no advantage is to be taken of her position.*

- *I'm one of the undeserving poor: thats what I am.*

- *Now, Mr Higgins, please dont say anything to make the girl conceited about herself.*

Act 3

- *If people would only be frank and say what they really think!*

- *The new small talk. You do it so awfully well.*

- *It's no use. I shall never be able to bring myself to use that word.*

- *But she's got some silly bee in her bonnet about Eliza. She keeps saying 'You don't think, sir': doesnt she, Pick?*

- *You certainly are a pair of pretty babies, playing with your live doll.*

Act 4

- *Why have you begun going on like this? May I ask whether you complain of your treatment here?*

- *You go to bed and have a good nice rest; and then get up and look at yourself in the glass; and you wont feel so cheap.*

- *We'll drive about all night; and in the morning I'll call on old Mrs Higgins and ask her what I ought to do.*

Act 5

- *Who asked him to make a gentleman of me?*

- *I dont think you quite realize what anything in the nature of brain work means to a girl of her class.*

- *So glad to see you again, Colonel Pickering... Quite chilly this morning, isnt it?*

- *You musnt mind that. Higgins takes off his boots all over the place.*

- *... I know I can be a lady to you, because you always treat me as a lady, and always will.*

- *I cant change my nature; and I dont intend to change my manners.*

2   Now write down some of your favourite lines or speeches from the play. Note who said them and try to explain why you thought they were effective. Perhaps they were amusing or sad or dramatic?

3   Compare your choices with a partner. Listen to what the other person has chosen and discuss the reasons for each of your choices.

Secondary characters

In a play or novel there are usually some main characters (also known as *principal* or *primary* characters) and other characters who are important – sometimes very important – but whom you could not describe as the main ones. These are known as the *secondary* characters.

MRS PEARCE
She appears on pages 21-49 and has a lot to say to both Eliza and Higgins. She is also referred to later by Higgins on page 63.

ALFRED DOOLITTLE
You may think he is a main character. Look at pages 39-49 and pages 85-97.

MRS HIGGINS
Look at pages 51-66 and pages 83-105.

PICKERING
Look at pages 10-18, pages 21-32, pages 35-50, pages 55-74, pages 84-97.

THE EYNSFORD HILL FAMILY
Mrs Eynsford Hill pages 7-15 and pages 54-62
Clara pages 7-15 and pages 54-62
Freddy pages 7-18 and pages 55-61

4   Choose one or two of the following and write:

- a conversation Mrs Pearce has with another housekeeper about the events at the Higgins house;

- your opinion as to why these secondary characters (above) are used in the play;
- the speech Doolittle might have to make to the Wannafeller Moral Reform League (see pages 85-8);
- a series of letters Mrs Higgins might write to a friend about her son and Eliza;
- an essay on the importance of all of these characters in *Pygmalion*.

Behaviour and morals

☐ Look at the following spider graph.

It gives examples of the behaviour of characters or their attitudes to life. There are only a few examples on this graph. Copy it out and add as many other points as you can.

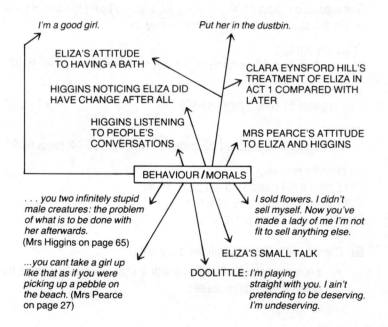

I'm a good girl.

Put her in the dustbin.

ELIZA'S ATTITUDE TO HAVING A BATH

CLARA EYNSFORD HILL'S TREATMENT OF ELIZA IN ACT 1 COMPARED WITH LATER

HIGGINS NOTICING ELIZA DID HAVE CHANGE AFTER ALL

HIGGINS LISTENING TO PEOPLE'S CONVERSATIONS

MRS PEARCE'S ATTITUDE TO ELIZA AND HIGGINS

BEHAVIOUR / MORALS

. . . you two infinitely stupid male creatures: the problem of what is to be done with her afterwards. (Mrs Higgins on page 65)

I sold flowers. I didn't sell myself. Now you've made a lady of me I'm not fit to sell anything else.

...you cant take a girl up like that as if you were picking up a pebble on the beach. (Mrs Pearce on page 27)

ELIZA'S SMALL TALK

DOOLITTLE: I'm playing straight with you. I ain't pretending to be deserving. I'm undeserving.

[2] When you have done this – you ought to be able to add at least a dozen examples of your own – share your ideas with others. Have a brain-storming session to help you find ideas.

[3] Use all the notes you make for an essay: *How people behave in Shaw's Pygmalion*.

You could look at these points:
- characters who appear to behave properly;
- characters who seem cruel to others;
- views in the play about how people should behave;
- different scenes where behaving properly is important.

Money and class

[1] As in the work looking at behaviour and morals on page 138 try to do the same with the themes of money and class. Copy out this diagram and add more of your own ideas and examples from the play.

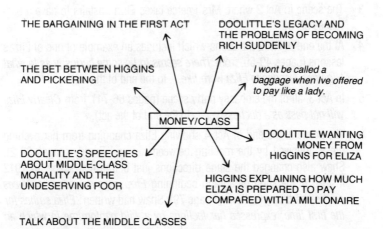

THE BARGAINING IN THE FIRST ACT

DOOLITTLE'S LEGACY AND THE PROBLEMS OF BECOMING RICH SUDDENLY

THE BET BETWEEN HIGGINS AND PICKERING

I wont be called a baggage when Ive offered to pay like a lady.

MONEY/CLASS

DOOLITTLE WANTING MONEY FROM HIGGINS FOR ELIZA

DOOLITTLE'S SPEECHES ABOUT MIDDLE-CLASS MORALITY AND THE UNDESERVING POOR

HIGGINS EXPLAINING HOW MUCH ELIZA IS PREPARED TO PAY COMPARED WITH A MILLIONAIRE

TALK ABOUT THE MIDDLE CLASSES

[2] Now write about the importance of money in *Pygmalion*, using incidents from the play and what the different characters think and say about money.

Different versions of the play

Shaw wrote *Pygmalion* in 1912. The version of *Pygmalion* in this edition is the one Shaw revised for the 1938 film. He changed some dialogues and added completely new scenes which could be used in the film. Here is a list of Shaw's additions to the 1912 version:

1 Part of the Preface where Shaw gives instructions for technicians, and the point he makes in the second paragraph (page 1) about the English being unable to spell.

2 The short scene where Eliza takes a taxi home and is then seen in her room (pages 18-19). The taxi cab had appeared in the 1912 version but the dialogue was much shorter with Eliza giving the driver directions to where she lived. She had then slammed the door and the scene had ended with Freddy saying *Well, I'm dashed!* There had been no real conversation between Eliza and the driver and no glimpse of Eliza at home in 1912.

3 The scene in Act 2 where Mrs Pearce takes Eliza upstairs to have a bath (pages 32-5).

4 At the end of Act 2 the scene which includes an example of one of Eliza's lessons (pages 49-50, from *There seems to be some curiosity as to what Higgins's lessons to Eliza were like...* to the end of the act).

5 In Act 3, all of the embassy party scene (pages 66-71), from *Clearly Eliza will not pass as a duchess yet...* to the end of the act).

6 The scene at the end of Act 4 showing Eliza changing from her evening dress, followed by the meeting between her and Freddy (pages 80-2). Shaw also changed the stage directions just before that scene. In 1912 instead of the short paragraph beginning *Eliza goes down on her knees on the heartthrug* (bottom of page 79), Shaw had written: *Eliza smiles for the first time; expresses her feelings by a wild pantomime in which an*

imitation of Higgins's exit is confused with her own triumph; and finally goes down on her knees on the hearthrug to look for the ring.

7   Shaw changed the very ending of the play. In 1912, instead of the last few lines beginning:

> LIZA   [disdainfully] *Number eights are too small for you...*
>
> pages 104-5

Shaw had written the following:

> LIZA   [disdainfully] *Buy them yourself.* (She sweeps out.)
>
> MRS HIGGINS   *I'm afraid you've spoiled that girl Henry. But never mind, dear: I'll buy you the tie and gloves.*
>
> HIGGINS   [sunnily] *Oh don't bother. She'll buy 'em all right enough. Goodbye.*
>
> They kiss, Mrs Higgins runs out. Higgins, left alone, rattles his cash in his pockets; chuckles; and disports himself in a highly self-satisfied manner.

1   Look carefully at all these additions and changes made by Shaw for the revised edition of *Pygmalion*.

- Discuss what you think they add to the play.
- Write down all the advantages each addition has for the meaning and success of the whole play.

Remember Shaw did *not* want audiences to think that there would be a romantic ending between Eliza and Higgins.

If you get a chance, watch either the original 1938 film version, starring Leslie Howard and Wendy Hiller, or the stage musical, *My Fair Lady* (see Introduction, page xi) which was filmed. In the film of *My Fair Lady,* apart from the addition of many songs, there are changes from the original play:

- a scene at the Ascot races (instead of Mrs Higgins's at-home day), in which Eliza shocks everyone there by some very colourful language shouting for a horse to move faster;

- an extended language lesson scene which includes Eliza eventually changing from saying *The rine in Spine sties minely in the pline* to *The rain in Spain stays mainly in the plain.*
- Doolittle preparing to get married;
- more scenes with Freddy.

Also in *My Fair Lady* the ending is much more romantic: Eliza has promised to marry Freddy but when Higgins is alone listening to the sound of her voice on his machinery she re-enters. Higgins looks content and simply asks where his slippers are. Eliza then cries and stays. Not a dry eye in the cinema!!

2 Look at some lines of the songs used in *My Fair Lady.* Can you work out which character sang which?

1 *Why can't the English teach their children how to speak?*

2 *Wouldn't it be loverly?* (The first line starts *All I want is a room somewhere far away from the cold night air.*)

3 *Just you wait 'enry 'iggins, just you wait.*

4 *I'm getting married in the morning... Get me to the church on time.*

5 *Why can't a woman be more like a man?*

6 *Show me.*

7 *I've grown accustomed to her face.*

8 *On the street where you live.*

9 *I could have danced all night.*

10 *I'm an ordinary man.*

3 When you have worked out the characters (answers on page 154), see if you can decide with others just where in the play the songs might fit.

Staging the play

If you had to cast the play for a performance what sort of actor or actress would be right for each part? The three most famous combinations playing

Eliza and Higgins have been Mrs Patrick Campbell and Herbert Tree, Wendy Hiller and Leslie Howard, Julie Andrews (stage) or Audrey Hepburn (film) and Rex Harrison.

You should be able to find pictures of all these actors but they may not match your image of the characters.

☐ Draw up a chart of the characters in the play and then a list of qualities you would look for when casting. These qualities can be wide ranging - from physical appearance to the way an actor should play the part.

Remember to check Shaw's own stage directions when each character makes his or her first appearance.

Sequels

Shaw felt he had to write an epilogue so that all readers knew exactly what his intentions were for all the characters. Read it through. You may feel that if you had the chance you would not have that ending. Think about what could happen to the characters.

1️⃣ Write your own sequel to the play. You can do this in ordinary prose but see if you can continue the play using as much of Shaw's style and the characters' voices and actions as possible.

If you want, keep the ideas that Shaw has in his epilogue; otherwise you can change them and substitute your own. Whatever you decide, remember the following points if you are going to continue by writing in play form:

- you must decide how many scenes you are going to write;
- what has happened to the characters right up to Shaw's ending;
- the style of the dialogue (Higgins would speak in a different way from Eliza or Freddy and so on);
- whether some of the smaller characters might make more appearances (for example Mrs Pearce, Pickering, Clara);

143

- the importance of convincing stage directions (keep in mind Shaw's directions), especially those which help the reader see the way in which a character says something.

When you set out your play check how to write the play form by looking over the presentation in this edition.

2 Act out your sequel with others. This will need some rehearsal time. One of the groups will have to direct you.

If you have a lot of time for this try to research the period of the play to see what people wore in 1912. Shaw gives a lot of set detail, especially at the start of Acts 2 and 3. You might be able to find some appropriate or even authentic props to help your play.

3 Use a video if you have the resources to film your sequel. Before you do this you will need to make a story/film board to note down what you intend to film, the action, dialogue and props used.

If other groups have written and performed their sequels watch them and then all of you decide which is the best and nearest to Shaw's own style.

4 The play has been set to music once. Do you think you could write lyrics and music for your own version?

Adding scenes

At some points in the play a certain amount of time elapses between one scene and another.

1 Write the following additional scenes where Eliza's thoughts become known. You can do this as a monologue (that is a speech just for Eliza, with no other characters), or you can have her talking to other characters as appropriate to the particular part of the play. When you are writing these scenes try to keep the style of Eliza's speech in mind so that your style can follow the play's as much as possible.

Scene 1: Eliza after she has returned home following Act 1 when she decides to go to Higgins to ask for lessons.

Scene 2: Eliza in the bathroom, after Mrs Pearce has left – before Eliza returns downstairs to see Higgins, Pickering and, of course, her father.

Scene 3: Eliza after she has left the at-home day of Mrs Higgins, following her outburst in Act 2.

Scene 4: Eliza's thoughts as she leaves the embassy party.

Scene 5: Eliza in her room at Higgins's house before she goes to meet Freddy following her argument with Higgins (after page 79 in this edition).

Scene 6: Eliza returning to meet some of her old friends in the Covent Garden area.

2 Imagine Eliza keeps up a correspondence with some of her friends during her time with Higgins. As a group, discuss the following points:

• What might she write?
• Would she reveal her true feelings?
• What does she think of Higgins?
• Does she really love Freddy?
• Were the at-home day and the embassy party very difficult for her?

How the characters develop

Eliza Doolittle

Eliza changes a lot by the end of the play – and not just in the way she speaks. Here are some of the things she says at different stages of the play:

• *I'm a good girl, I am.*

pages 13, 29, 31, 47

• *He's no right to take away my character. My character is the same to me as any lady's.*

page 14

- *You ought to be stuffed with nails, you ought... Take the whole blooming basket for sixpence.*

  page 17

- *If I'd known what I was letting myself in for, I wouldnt have come here. I always been a good girl; and I never offered to say a word to him; and I dont owe him nothing; and I dont care; and I wont be put upon; and I have my feelings the same as anyone else –*

  page 32

- *Aint you going to call me Miss Doolittle any more?*

  page 48

- *Ive won your bet for you, havent I? Thats enough for you. I dont matter, I suppose.*

  page 75

- *Your calling me Miss Doolittle that day when I first came to visit Wimpole Street. That was the beginning of self-respect for me.*

  page 93

- *...the difference between a lady and a flower girl is not how she behaves but how she's treated. I shall always be a flower girl to Professor Higgins, because he always treats me as a flower girl, and always will; but I know I can be a lady to you, because you always treat me as a lady, and always will.*

  pages 93-4

- *You know I cant go back to the gutter, as you call it, and that I have no real friends in the world but you and the Colonel.*

  page 102

- *You cant take away the knowledge you gave me... That's done you, Enry Iggins, it az.*

  page 103

1 Look carefully at these quotations from the play and, with a partner, find more quotations and further points where you think Eliza has something important to say. Remember her main scenes:

- selling flowers
- asking Higgins for lessons
- having a bath

- meeting her father
- the lesson
- Mrs Higgins's at-home day
- the embassy party
- back with Higgins after the party
- with Freddy
- seeing Higgins again after she has run away

Note down how she behaves in each of the scenes.

2 When you have made notes on her speeches and actions use all your information to write an essay on the character of Eliza with the title: *In what ways does Eliza Doolittle change in Pygmalion?*

Use examples from the play and quotations in this essay.

Henry Higgins

At the beginning of the play Henry Higgins appears as just a figure in the crowd but soon makes his presence felt. He has no hesitation in telling Eliza just what he thinks about her and throughout the play seems to treat her like an object. The following quotations give us an idea of his view on things:

- *Well sir, in three months I could pass that girl off as a duchess at an ambassador's garden party.*

page 16

- *It's handsome. By George, it's enormous! it's the biggest offer I ever had.*

page 25

- *You shouldnt cut your old friends now that you have risen in the world. That's what we call snobbery.*

page 48

- *You see, we're all savages, more or less. We're supposed to be civilized and cultured.*

page 56

- *If I hadnt backed myself to do it I should have chucked the whole thing up two months ago. It was a silly notion: the whole thing has been a bore.*

  page 73

- *I have created this thing out of the squashed cabbage leaves of Covent Garden; and now she pretends to play the fine lady with me.*

  page 92

- *The question is not whether I treat you rudely, but whether you ever heard me treat anyone else better.*

  page 98

- *Youve had a thousand times as much out of me as I have out of you.*

  page 99

- *If you cant appreciate what youve got, youd better get what you can appreciate.*

  page 102

3 As with the piece on Eliza look for more examples to show you the character of Higgins in different parts of the play. Look at his long speeches. In a group, write down examples which you think are most important. Let each member of the group take one act and then discuss your findings.

Use your notes for the following essay: *Discuss whether you feel Henry Higgins is really more concerned with Eliza or himself in **Pygmalion**.*

Alfred Doolittle

Look at two speeches made by Alfred Doolittle. The first one is from Act 2 (pages 43-4), when he meets Higgins for the first time. It begins:

Dont say that, Governor. Dont look at it that way. What am I, Governors both? I ask you, what am I? I'm one of the undeserving poor: thats what I am.

The second speech is in the last act (page 87), after Doolittle discovers he is a millionaire, and begins:

It aint the lecturing I mind. I'll lecture them blue in the face, I will, and not turn a hair. It's making a gentleman of me that I object to.

These are two long speeches – one when Doolittle has no money and the other when he suddenly has lots!

4 In a group, assign the following tasks to each member of the group:

1 Make a list of all the things Doolittle felt he could do as a member of the *undeserving poor* in the first speech.

2 Note down all the words or phrases he repeats in the first speech.

3 Look at the rest of Doolittle's speeches in Act 2 and note down anything that you think helps to reveal his thoughts and character.

4 Make a list of all the problems he has come across since he became rich. (Remember *touched for* means being asked for money).

5 Look at the other speeches on pages 86-8 and note down any other problems Doolittle feels he has.

5 Try learning one of these speeches – it will give you an idea of Shaw's rhythm and style and of how difficult it may be for an actor.

Extension assignments

1 As a whole group, write down the advantages and disadvantages of becoming rich very suddenly. You could enlarge this idea by making it into a full-scale debate with written speeches for both sides of the argument.

2 As a group, plan together and then write a piece on whether you feel there is the same division of classes in England today as Doolittle thought there was in 1912.

3 You have been asked to design a book cover for a new edition of *Pygmalion*.
   • Design the cover.

- Write the blurb for the back cover.
- Design a promotional handout which would be sent to people to try to get them to buy the book.

4 Look back at the section on critical reaction in the Introduction (pages xiii-xv). The newspapers had a lot to write about for the first performance of *Pygmalion*.

Write your own review of the play, including something about the play as a whole, the characters, dialogue, ending and so on. If you have seen a performance of the play or one of the films, then of course include comments about that as well.

5 Look up the events of 1912, the year in which the play is set. Check over the Introduction, go to the library, see if you can find old papers. The Longman Twentieth Century Chronicle is a useful resource. Write the story of Eliza for the front page of a newspaper of the day.

Choose your headline from those below or make up your own, and design a front page that might have covered the story. Remember another big event of 1912 was the sinking of the ship The Titanic – you may need that on your front page as well.

- Flower girl hits the heights
- Higgins does it again
- East End meets West End
- Shock! Horror! Foul language used at tea party

6 Prepare a speech for a radio or television programme where guests have to choose a favourite book or play and talk about it. You choose *Pygmalion*.

7 Write your own play or story based on the idea of someone trying to change the lifestyle of another person. Base this on the plot of *Pygmalion* or think of something entirely different.

Suggestion for further reading

A selection of other plays by George Bernard Shaw

Androcles and the Lion
Set in Roman times about a man who pulls out a thorn from an injured lion and then finds the lion befriends him. Often performed by schools.

Major Barbara
A Salvation Army Major is faced with the problem of her father's job which is making ammunition for wars.

Arms and the Man
An anti-war play set in central Europe in the last century – often performed by schools.

Saint Joan
A different look at the story of Joan of Arc, Maid of Orleans, who led the French in battle against the English and was burned as a witch In 1431.

Mrs Warren's Profession
A serious look at hypocrisy in society – dealing with earning money by prostitution.

You Never Can Tell
An amusing play about a family who find out about the past of its members – the most important part is for the waiter in this play.

Works exploring similar themes to *Pygmalion*

One of the most obvious stories is the ballet *Coppelia*, which is about a dollmaker who creates a doll so life-like it looks like a real woman. The man is tricked when he *thinks* his doll comes alive.

The Taming of the Shrew   by Shakespeare
Petruchio tries to 'tame' the fiery Katherina in order to make her become his obedient wife.

Frankenstein   by Mary Shelley
Frankenstein constructs a monster and gives it life.

Hobson's Choice by Harold Brighouse
A timid shoemaker is helped by the woman he eventually marries.

Trilby by George du Maurier
Nineteenth-century novel about a famous singer whose talent depends on the mesmeric influence of Svengali, a musician. A serious book in which there are tragic consequences.

I Know Why the Caged Bird Sings by Maya Angelou
Part of a trilogy of books depicting the author's development from a girl to a woman through a difficult childhood.

Novels including interesting uses of dialect

Roots by Arnold Wesker
Play about a woman trying to break away from the conventions of her family. The heroine – like Eliza – is educated by a man and then discovers her independent self.

The Color Purple by Alice Walker
A young girl having to grow up amidst degradation and difficulties.

Oliver Twist and *Great Expectations* by Charles Dickens
These, and many other wonderful books by this great author, include extremely carefully described people and very realistic dialogue.

Cider with Rosie by Laurie Lee
The story of a young boy growing up in the Cotswolds.

To Kill A Mockingbird by Harper Lee
Set in the deep South of America, depicting racial prejudice amongst a community where a white lawyer attempts to defend a black man falsely accused of rape.

Dialect poetry

The Guidwife of Wauchope-House to Robert Burns (1787); *Epistle to Captain William Logan; Epistle from a Taylor* by Robert Burns
A Collier's Wife; Violets by D H Lawrence

Dread Beat and Blood (Anthology); *Sonny's lettah*   by Linton Kwesi Johnson

This is the six a clock news   by Tom Leonard

The Lion and Albert; The return of Albert   by Marriott Edgar

Wider reading assignments

1. When you have read at least one other play by Shaw look carefully at the main female character and compare her with Eliza Doolittle. Think about whether the character is as strong or has such forthright views.

2. From any Shaw plays you have read or seen can you find any themes in common with those of *Pygmalion*? What have you found interesting in other Shaw plays? Do you think the Shaw plays you have come across have relevance today?

3. If there has been one play of Shaw's that you have enjoyed particularly, write a short piece on why you liked the play and give a brief outline as well as your reasons for recommending it to a friend.

4. Read one of the novels or plays from the list in which one character is influenced by others. (Two of the novels are autobiographical.) Write a review of the play or novel chosen.
   - Do you think the main character changes for the better?
   - Can you think of any other books or plays you have read where characters are seen to be helped or hindered by others?

5. Read at least one of the books or plays written partly in dialect. Why do you think the author included passages in dialect?

   Write a letter to a friend recommending the novel or play of your choice.

6. Find as many dialect poems as you can in poetry anthologies. Choose any three and try to rewrite them in clear modern English – you might

need a dictionary or encyclopaedia to help, or use a good anthology which gives a glossary to the poems.

When you have rewritten the poems explain what makes the original version so effective.

My Fair Lady songs: answers from page 143

1 Higgins
2 Eliza
3 Eliza
4 Doolittle
5 Higgins
6 Eliza (singing to Freddy)
7 Higgins
8 Freddy
9 Eliza
10 Higgins